10/12

How To
Turn Your Marriage Around
in 10 Days
Philip Wagner

***What others are saying about "How To Turn Your
Marriage Around in 10 Days"***

*This is one of the best and most practical books on
marriage I have ever read. I underlined on every
page and it motivated me to put more energy into my
marriage. Philip Wagner packs an incredible wealth
of practical wisdom in this easy-to-read volume. If
you want to rekindle your relationship and keep your
marriage fresh then this book is for you. I devoured
it and will pass it on to friends. Philip Wagner writes
in such an authentic way. It's like sitting down with
a friend who inspires you to want to have a stronger
marriage.*

Jim Burns PhD
President, HomeWord
Author of Creating An Intimate Marriage and Closer

*Philip and Holly Wagner are, in my opinion, two of
the foremost voices for successful marriages in our
world today. Our church has benefitted hugely from
their investment in our marriages. I firmly believe
that this book's premise is true, you absolutely can
turn your marriage around in 10 days. Don't just
survive. Get it today!*

Dino Rizzo
Lead Pastor, Healing Place Church, Baton Rouge,
LA
Author of Servolution

Many books make promises. How To Turn Your Marriage Around in 10 Days delivers. With powerful insight, personal transparency, and potent inspiration, Phillip Wagner delivers a message that will revive your marriage and enable you to enjoy your life to the fullest.

Chris Hodges
Pastor, Church of the Highlands, Birmingham, Alabama
Author of "Fresh Air"

In 'How To Turn Your Marriage Around in Ten Days', Philip Wagner has given something to the state of marriage it desperately needs, hope. So many have lost hope for their marriage because they have bought into the belief that they just don't have what it takes to turn it around. This book dispels that lie. Representing that "simplicity the other side of complexity", this book is as powerful a turnaround tool as I have ever seen. In the hands of those needing a fresh start, this book will breathe hope, life, and I believe, the miracle of turnaround.

Dr. Robert Flores
President, Life Pacific College, San Dimas, California

I love to hear Philip teach on relationships. He and Holly are some of the most incredible people I've ever met, and I never cease to be amazed – or amused – in listening to them share their insight on the subject. *Philip has done an amazing job in writing a book that is full of relationship "gold", easy to read, engaging and extremely practical. This is a lifesaver for the person whose marriage is barely hanging on, but it's also a great resource to take a good marriage to the next level or provide insight for those who may not be married yet.*

John Siebeling
Lead Pastor, The Life Church, Memphis, TN

Philip Wagner's teachings are filled with great, practical wisdom and truths in the area of marriage. As his friend, I know he practices what he preaches. As a married man, I know what he says works! I truly believe this book will help you and your spouse live out God's heart for your marriage.

Robert Morris
Senior Pastor, Gateway Church
Bestselling author of *The Blessed Live, From Dream to Destiny, & The God I Never Knew*

I love being around Philip and Holly Wagner because their relationship is alive! Besides being amazing pastors, they have a lot to teach any couple about increasing the heart rate in their home. Whether your relationship needs CPR, or you are just looking for ways to improve it, Philip's book is for you! It's motivating . . . Practical . . . And the material in it works without exception. This is what I want to tell every married couple: "Get you some of this!"

Rick Bezet
Lead Pastor, New Life Church, Little Rock, Arkansas

Married couples tend to think that the challenges they face are unique to themselves and their situation. This book makes us realize that the problems are more common than we think. What Phillip has written not only gives us hope in facing those problems, he also shows us very simple and practical steps to turn any marriage around. This is a must-read, not only for couples with marriage problems, but for everyone interested in building a better marriage. I highly recommend it!

Jeffrey Rachmat
Senior Pastor, Jakarta Praise Community Church, Jakarta, Indonesia

Acknowledgments

⎯⎯∽∽∽⎯⎯

This is the part where I'm supposed to thank everybody. Is there a rule about these acknowledgments? Does anyone read this part of the book anyway? Well here's my best effort.

I want to thank the one person who not only believes in me, but also endured me continually talking about my ideas, my whining and my lack of follow through on my regular responsibilities. I'm talking, of course, about my wife, Holly, or as she's known to a few thousand people, @HollyWagnerLA. You are the love of my life, my friend, my encourager and an inspiration to me. Your passion is contagious and your energy is endless and it's the reason I drink double cappuccinos late into the afternoon. You made this book possible. Your encouragement inspires me.

Thank you Holly for sticking with me for 27 years of marriage, loving me, making changes in your heart and explaining to me those things that should have been obvious in the first place. Thank you for staying dedicated to our marriage, which has brought me strength, healing and given me plenty of stuff to write about. I'm proud to be called "Oh - you're Holly's husband!"

Thank you for making it clear to me that those "irreconcilable differences" are probably going to be there for a long time and that you are committed to me anyway. Forever. I still wish you'd let me finish my own sentences more often.

Thanks also to my writing friends and partners, Steve Parolini and Ashley Abercrombie. This book would only be marginally readable, if it weren't for your contribution. I still think you were wrong about deleting the introduction, changing the POV, and re-writing the entire book in your voice. Just kidding. All your advice was brilliant. You deserve a raise, a vacation and/or some therapy. I also want to thank anyone else I may have forgotten, who made some suggestions that I am still confident were my idea.

Thank you to my kids Jordan and Paris, who are grown now and are busy doing their own stuff and probably didn't even know I was working on this book.

How is this going so far? Are you still with me? Just a few more to go.

Thank you to everybody who wrote about marriage, which apparently is a lot of people. But the guys who impacted me the most are: Dr. Neil Clark Warren, Gary Smalley, Emerson Eggerichs and Dr. Jim Burns (who I knew before he was "Dr. Jim" – and knew nothing about marriage or relationships ...or dating for that matter because we were in high school).

Who else should I thank? I guess it's a little random but I want to thank that overly energetic barista at Starbucks who kept bringing more Cappuccinos to help me keep writing.

And lastly, I want to thank Rascal Flatts, Lady Antebellum, Billy Joel and Paul McCartney who did not help me with marriage tips but they but did write some pretty awesome love songs. I want to thank Michael Jordan for teaching me something about honor. (I'll explain later)

Above all, thanks to God, who without His grace I would have messed up my marriage, as well as many other things in life.

Well that should cover it. Hope you enjoy the book.

Table of Contents

Introduction
The Difference

—ᴗᴥᴗ—

Our marriage was going to be different.

I had been listening to the wisdom, the warnings and the time-tested advice. "Marriage takes work," they said. I was not afraid of a little work.

Besides, we *were* different. We loved each other – a lot. We were not going to struggle like other couples. We would not lose the spark, we would not develop unrealistic expectations, we would not say hurtful things, or if we did, we surely would not let the sun go down on our anger. Our marriage was going to be better than anyone else's.

I was not so naïve to think the Beatles had nailed the truth with "all you need is love." I was smarter than that. I knew the real truth: all you need is *enough* love.

So while the kind-hearted and broken-hearted offered their wisdom, warnings and time-tested advice, we stood tall before God and man, certain we had more than enough love. Ours would be the marriage against which to judge all other marriages.

Turns out we were *exactly* like everyone else.

We had unrealistic expectations. We underestimated the amount of work a marriage takes. We discovered that even a loving, generous, kind-hearted person could be a real jerk sometimes.

We realized that in order to have a great marriage, we would need to do what every other successful couple did...

>*Work at it.*
>*Embrace change.*
>*Grow up.*

Realization was just the first step. The second – and this is most important step – was doing something about it.

You have probably heard all kinds of scary statistics about marriage. For example, according to author and Psychologist, Kevin Lehman, the average marriage in America lasts seven years. That is far from the "forever" we agree to in the wedding ceremony. Dr. Neil Clark Warren tells of an even more staggering statistic, stating that "200,000 marriages will end this year that did not make it to the second anniversary."

Granted, some of the statistics we hear these days like *"50% of marriages end in divorce"* are blown out of proportion and unsubstantiated and end up producing either exaggerated fears or a sense of hopelessness that is unfounded.

Do you know what I believe is the greatest threat to marriage today?

It is us! We just do not know how to do it right.

Reading this book puts you in a special category of people – people who are not afraid of admitting their marriage needs work. You could be one of those people who simply wants to make a good thing great! Maybe you are noticing you have lost that lovin' feeling, or maybe you are staring the D-word in the face. Wherever you are along that continuum, you know your marriage is not what it could be, should be.

People who make the effort to understand what is not working in their marriage are a rare breed. People who make genuine changes in their attitudes and actions are rarer still.

Welcome to rarified air.

The single most important relationship anyone will have in this life is marriage. Yet so many people never read a single thing about how to do it right. We think our love will be enough. We think we will just figure it out, or that problems will solve themselves.

Then we hit a wall. Something feels broken. Something is not right. We may still say, "I love you," every morning, but secretly we are angry, tired, frustrated, lonely.

We need help!

A few years ago, I went to traffic school. This may have had something to do with my driving. Let's just say attendance was not optional and leave it at that.

I drive every day. (It's a California thing.) I rely on my driving skill for my work, my family and my life. I thought I knew all I needed to know about driving, but soon after the class started I was surprised to discover just how many things I did not know or had forgotten.

> *What is the difference between a double yellow line and a broken white line?*
> *How many feet before an intersection should you signal?*
> *What do all these different traffic signs mean?*

Did you know that having a Driver's License is a privilege and not a right? I'm pretty sure I had not thought of that prior to traffic school.

If I wanted to pass the test at the end of the class, I needed to know these answers.

This got me thinking... What if we married couples had to take a quiz every five years in order to renew our marriage licenses? Would we remember what we are supposed to be doing? How to avoid unnecessary conflict? How to resolve differences? What it means to love unconditionally? Would we remember that trust is a privilege and not a right?

How well would we recognize all the different signs?

It does not matter if you have been married twenty months or twenty years, there is always a good reason to learn what makes a marriage work. Whether you are here because you have run a few red lights in your relationship, or because it is a total wreck, I want to welcome you and offer you this simple encouragement: *You can turn your marriage around!*

In the chapters that follow, I am going to give you some ideas for ten different areas of your marriage relationship. On **Day One**, focus on the topic in that chapter. Give the topic your complete attention from sunup to sundown. Embrace the ideas and wisdom with gusto.

Go all in.

On **Day Two**, do the same with the second chapter. Continue until you have gone through every chapter. In ten days, you could turn your marriage around, or at the very least, you will have created the right environment for a thriving marriage rather than one that is merely surviving.

This works. It is simple, the chapters are not long, the advice is not complicated, but that does not mean it is easy. Growth demands vulnerability and trust. You will experience uncomfortable emotions. You will face resistance. You may even question if you are getting anything out of this process, but if you give the biblically-based truths in this book a chance, I guarantee you will see a change.

Do you want a great relationship? Do you want a marriage that flourishes? You can have what so many couples are missing and what the best ones already know.

Put your heart and soul into this and you will not be disappointed.

First, a word of clarification: This is not a list of ten things to "fix and forget." Each of the ten days is about embracing real change. Each day you will be challenged to take a hard look at current behaviors and habits and turn them around, one by one. This is not a magic pill; it is a reframing. Do not leave behind or forget on Day Five what you may have learned on Day Two.

I am going to start by sharing a little secret. This is the foundation for everything that follows: *Focus*.

Focus on meeting the needs of your spouse. While no person can meet every need of their spouse, the important needs in a marriage can be met by the attitude we have and how we approach the relationship.

Instead of approaching this royal relationship mainly from the, "What can you do for me?" perspective, we can begin to turn things around by thinking, "How can I help bring out the best in you?" or "How can I bring a serving attitude into our relationship that will produce a healthy love and respect for each other?"

In order to discover a healthy way to serve each other some marriages may have to work through the hindrances of our past. I have observed many relationships in which one partner has expectations of their spouse that are unreasonable, demeaning or dysfunctional. I'm not suggesting that you serve these unhealthy expectations.

I am suggesting that you focus on meeting the appropriate human needs of your spouse by serving them with honor.

Consider these words from Matthew:

> *The Son of Man did not come to be served, but to serve*. (Matthew 20:28)

And these words about marriage from the Apostle Paul:

> *Submit to one another out of reverence for Christ.* (Ephesians 5:21)

Consider this:

In what ways can I serve my spouse and our marriage?

How can we serve each other with honor and respect?

When asked to share the greatest example of love in the arts, we often point to Shakespeare's Romeo and Juliet. On the surface, it seems like the perfect choice. It is a story of great love, but we sort of gloss over that whole tragic aspect, don't we? Romeo and Juliet is all about passion and emotion. Truly successful relationships are about a different kind of love – the kind demonstrated in a much different artistic work, *Schindler's List.* Yes, *Schindler's List.* True love is all about sacrifice. Love may need to be expressed by drastic choices and uncommon investment.

As you spend time in the pages of this book, I invite you to return to your first love. Remember the desire, trust and passion that brought you together in the first place. Remember the dedication, and then open your heart and mind to a more mature kind of love – a love far beyond your wildest expectations.

A great marriage is worth the work.

King Solomon has a few things to say about marriage. While he is speaking to husbands in the following passage, the greater message is true for wives as well.

> *May your fountain be blessed, and may you rejoice in the wife of your youth. A loving doe, a graceful deer—may her breasts satisfy you always, may you ever be intoxicated with her love.* (Proverbs 5:18-19)

Don't you just love the Bible!

May you ever be intoxicated. What a powerful marriage blessing and it comes not from a secret rendezvous or a swallowing of poison, but discovering how to love deeply, honestly...how to love sacrificially.

Let's get started.

[A brief note for those of you who are not married – there is great wisdom here for you, too. While some of the content is directed specifically to married couples, much of the underlying truth is applicable to other relationships, including that romantic one you are in right now. File the marriage-specific content away for your future reference, but do not miss the rest of the wisdom. While I will be speaking directly to married couples on these pages, I am thinking of you too.]

Day One:
Priorities

The main thing is to keep the main thing the main thing.
- Stephen Covey

Wherever your treasure is, there the desires of your heart will also be.
- Jesus Christ

A hundred years from now, historians will be studying you and me, trying to understand what made us tick, what made us do the things we did.

Imagine for a moment that those researchers happened upon your calendar, your checkbook, or your budget spreadsheet. What would they conclude after studying these documents?

I know what you are thinking…so go ahead, satisfy your curiosity. Open up your calendar, your checkbook and your budget spreadsheet.

Now put on the historian's hat.

Where do you spend your money? How do you spend your time? Be honest with yourself about the trends you observe. Is the budgeted amount for "entertainment" smaller than the one for "car maintenance"?

What are your goals?

Where we spend our time and how we spend our money usually reveals our priorities. Our priorities define us.

If your calendar is filled with dinner parties and social events, then we can reasonably assume that spending time with friends is important to you. If you spend your money at movie theaters, bookstores, and sporting events, entertainment is probably high on your list.

Okay, time for a reality check: where does your marriage land on your list of priorities? I know there is no line item for "marriage expenses," but with a little creative thinking it is pretty easy to determine.

Does prioritizing time with friends speak about your spouse's needs and wants, or yours? Do your checkbook entries reveal money spent growing your relationship, or escaping it?

What is the priority of your life?

Is your marriage business-centered? Children-centered? Friend-centered? Ministry-centered? Or is your marriage itself the priority?

A marriage-centered life is all about putting marriage first. This is not something we usually think about. We are not intentional about our marriages – certainly not at first. We think our love is enough. We think love *is* our marriage.

We are not to make our spouse an 'idol' above all others or even above our faith in God; but because of our faith in God and our values in life, we make the conscious decision not to 'neglect' our marriage by letting it slip way down the "important priorities list."

However, there is so much more to marriage. I had just finished speaking to a group about this very topic when a woman came up to me, clearly moved by the message.

"Thank you so much for teaching about the marriage-centered life," she said. "We really needed to hear this. My husband and I haven't gone out on a date night since our daughter was born."

I smiled, remembering vividly the challenges of my own marriage during the child-rearing years, and asked how old her daughter was.

"Ten," she said, without a hint of irony.

Wow! Ten years between date nights. I do not think that anyone goes into a marriage thinking they will have to endure such a long season of going without dates, but it does not happen all at once. It starts with one postponement of a dinner. "I really need to finish this project." Then a movie date bites the dust. "I am just too tired, tonight." A month of missed dates turns into six months, six months turns into a year, a year turns into ten and, broken by heartbreak and loneliness, they both wonder what happened to their marriage.

Holly and I struggled in the first few years of our marriage. It did not take long to move from the honeymoon period into the battle for supremacy. We disagreed, we argued, we hurt each other's feelings. Our differences were huge. I thought about her shortcomings every day. I focused on her mistakes and negative statements. I even entertained the *Thought That Must Not Be Uttered*, "I think I married the wrong person."

I had been a pastor for just eight months longer than I had been a husband and I was struggling with both. In the midst of these challenges – do not laugh– I had to give marriage counseling to two different couples. It is not like I could say "no," it was my job.

Needless to say, this initially compounded my marital angst. I needed help with my marriage and there I was tasked with giving advice to others, but then an amazing thing happened.

After listening to the horrible things these couples were saying to each other, I realized that my marriage was not in such dire shape after all. Sure, we had had disagreements, but these couples were not just disagreeing, they were in the midst of war. After hearing one couple tell of their awful behavior toward each other, I thought, perhaps a bit selfishly, "Holly and I had never behaved that way toward each other."

Focus on the Positives!

Over the course of two one-hour marriage-counseling sessions, I learned that I had a much better marriage than I had thought. Hearing about the difficulties those two couples were facing forced me to take a closer look at the negative things I had been thinking and feeling. When I did this, I discovered I had a pretty good wife. No, she was an *awesome* wife, with a ton of great qualities.

Bingo!

I started focusing on those great qualities. They had always been there, but I had forgotten about them because I was stupidly focusing on all the things I did not like about her instead.

My wife began to focus on my good traits too. (At the time, I was pretty sure this was a really long list, topped by humility, of course. I have since learned the error of my ways.)

This new way of thinking was a game changer! Our marriage momentum immediately turned away from decay and disappointment toward health and happiness.

What we focus on has our affection. When we make marriage a priority, we quickly learn to focus on seeing the good in one another, on giving attention to things that build up rather than tear down.

What we focus on, we bring power to. What happens when we focus on the positive aspects of our relationship? We begin to see that we are on the same team. We begin to see that both our similarities and differences can make us an even *better* team.

Focusing on the positives does not mean pretending we are perfect. We still need to address challenges and disagreements and other important issues. However, the lesson here – and this is what I discovered in those two hours of counseling others – is that what we focus on in our lives we will magnify.

Think back to when you first fell in love. Did you see only the negative things? I will bet you barely saw any of those at all, so stunned as you were by all the glowing, positive qualities. Well, those qualities are still there. Admittedly, they may be obscured by negative fault-finding, but they have not disappeared. To turn your marriage around, you need to start seeing the positive qualities, acknowledging them, and enjoying them.

You may be familiar with the parable of the lost sheep. It is a story Jesus tells about a man who owns one hundred sheep. One day the man realizes one sheep is missing. Not twenty or ten or even five. Just one sheep! The shepherd does not say, "Oh well, I still have ninety-nine," and leave it at that. Instead, he leaves the ninety-nine and goes looking for the one that is lost.

While the main point of this parable is about God's great love for the lost, there is a secondary message, one that is particularly applicable to marriage: When something of great value is lost, it is worth setting everything else aside to find it. Your marriage is something of great value!

If you have lost what you first knew – the love that brought both of you to the altar before God

29

– set everything else aside and search for it. Make your marriage the priority it was meant to be.

Think about what takes your attention away from your marriage. Is it your career, money, friends, hobbies, or goals? Is it your ministry or Church?

How will you prioritize your relationship? What will you give up in order to have a marriage-centered life? Start doing those things today.

Then consider the way you think about your spouse. Do you focus on her negative qualities? Turn that around. It is time to remember what brought you together and focus on your spouse's greatest qualities.

This does not mean that you are to act desperate. Do not suffocate your partner with an avalanche of words. Just change your focus.

Statistics reveal that the way marriage is done in America is not working. Nevertheless, if you do what others will not do you can have what others will not, a lasting, satisfying, and beautiful marriage.

Make Your Marriage a Priority!

Day One is about making your marriage a priority.

In the movie, *Crazy, Stupid, Love*, we watch two people make horrible decisions, go through all kinds of chaos, and consider all kinds of stupid ideas only to arrive at a poignant scene set in a familiar venue for spousal confrontations – a car. The husband, played by Steve Carrell, tells his wife, "I should have worked harder. I should have fought for you." He gave up too easy. He let his hurt feelings and shattered ego drive her away.

It is time to fight for your marriage; not to fight with your spouse. Stand up, focus on your marriage and make love your priority.

Are you ready to make this your priority today? Good. Then you are ready for **Day Two**.

Takeaways

List three things that stood out to you in this chapter:
1.
2.
3.

Prayer

Pray this prayer before taking the next step:

"Lord, help me to make our marriage the most important thing in my actions and thoughts today. Show me what I can do to make love the priority in my marriage. Forgive me for letting other things become more important. Help me to communicate to my spouse that our marriage is the most important element of my life."

Actions

What specific things will you do today to work on your priorities?

- _____
- _____
- _____

Day Two:
Honor

Better to die ten thousand deaths than wound my honor.
– Joseph Addison

A prophet is honored everywhere except in his own hometown and among his relatives and his own family.
– Jesus Christ

I get no respect. I told my psychiatrist that everyone hates me. He said I was being ridiculous – everyone doesn't know me yet.
– Rodney Dangerfield

D_o you remember your vows? You know, those words you said before God and everyone the day you got married. You do not? Me neither. I had to look mine up. You would have been really impressed if I had remembered them, wouldn't you?

So would Holly.

About those vows, did yours say anything like, "I promise to love, honor, respect and serve you through sickness and health till death do us part"?

Any of that ring a bell?

A vow is not something to be taken lightly. It is a sacred promise, or in the case of traditional marriage vows, a *series* of sacred promises, spoken before God and man, not because you want to make all the women cry and all the men nervous, but because you mean every word of it.

That "till death" promise is a big one. Based on those divorce statistics, it is apparently a bit too big for many couples. Want to know a secret? The answer to many of those couples' problems can be found right there in the same vow, nestled up against the promise of forever.

It is that word, "honor."

"To honor" means to show high respect for a person's worth, merit, or rank. The Bible is pretty clear about the role honor ought to play in relationships.

> *Be devoted to one another in love. Honor one*
> *another above yourselves.*
> (Romans 12:10)

This sounds a little like your marriage vow, doesn't it? Your job – no, your privilege – as husband or wife is to meet your spouse's deepest need. For many, that deepest need is honor.

We are not a very honoring society. We are quick to judge and blame and point out everything that is wrong with a person, but slow to celebrate or even acknowledge a person's worth. Sadly, this is just as true in our Christian culture as it is in the world at large.

In a world dominated by self-centered thinking, honoring does not come easy.

If your relationship is going south, I believe it is because you are missing honor. Perhaps you are not being honored. Maybe you are not showing honor to your spouse.

Honor is often revealed by how we speak about our spouse to others. However, honor begins at home and it is rooted in love and respect.

> *Each one of you also must love his wife as he*
> *loves himself, and the wife must respect her*
> *husband.* (Ephesians 5:33)

All of us, men and women alike, need to feel loved *and* respected, but as alluded to in this scripture, there are some subtle (and not so subtle in some cases) differences between the two sexes: Men tend to yearn for respect above everything else. They feel honored when they are respected. Women, on the other hand, experience honor when they feel loved.

Of course, each person is unique, so your wife may ache for respect, or your husband, love. The key is to understand what makes them feel most honored and to give that freely.

That word "freely" is important here. When we tie our gifts of respect and love to performance, we are not honoring the other person. When we use a scorecard to keep track of the things worthy of respect and love, we actually make our spouse feel *dis*-honored.

Honoring one another is an unconditional act. We honor our spouse for who they are, not focusing on who they are not. Once again, it is all about serving. (Do you see a trend developing here? Good.)

Every healthy and honoring relationship can be boiled down to moments when we are serving each other.

There is a scene in the movie *Jerry Maguire* that illustrates what honoring looks like. Tom Cruise plays the title character and Renee Zellweger plays Dorothy, the woman he falls for. After a whirlwind romance, they marry, but then she kicks him out because she does not believe he loves her. Time passes and lives go on, but then Jerry has an epiphany. This brings us to the climactic scene. It begins when Jerry walks boldly into their living room where Dorothy is sitting with a women's support group – a group defined by their disillusionment with men. Driven by passion and humility (and without a second thought about the less than sympathetic audience around his wife), he proceeds to apologize for his actions and express how much he loves her. Before he is even done with his heartfelt plea, Dorothy utters these words:

"Shut up. You had me at hello."

She said, in essence, "Stop talking, you already touched my heart." Wow. Isn't that something we all wish we could hear? Every man's dream conversation, "Say no more!"

Jerry had done plenty of selfish things in his life. One of the mistakes he had made was that he had not loved Dorothy deeply and sincerely – the very thing she longed for. However, in this scene he did just about everything right. It was not the exact words he spoke, although they were pretty good ("You complete me" wasn't half bad), it was the way he honored Dorothy in front of her peers.

It is natural for couples to go through different seasons in their marriage, but not all of the changes are positive. It is not uncommon for couples to shift from having desires – normal, God-given desires for attention and affection – to expectations. If we do not catch this shift soon enough, those expectations soon become demands, and this is what sends so many couples to counseling.

I am going to say it again, and I will keep saying it in these pages because the message is so critical to a healthy, happy relationship: Marriage is about meeting *your spouse's* deepest, realistic marital needs, not demanding that they meet yours.

Michael Jordan is the best basketball player who ever lived. I know what you are thinking, what does Michael Jordan have to do with honoring your spouse? Stick with me here. Michael Jordan is an icon. He is who Kobe and LeBron hope to be one day. (For the uninitiated, Kobe and LeBron are basketball players too. Good ones, but they are no Jordan.) He singlehandedly elevated the popularity of the sport. He was bigger than the game. He was the Beatles of basketball and…I got to meet him.

While Michael Jordan was shooting the film, *Space Jam*, here in Los Angeles, the studios erected a temporary basketball court in a tent. He used it to play games with college all-stars and other pro friends. My grand moment came after one of those pick-up games. I was so excited when a friend introduced us.

"Michael, Philip."
"Philip, Michael."

After the grand event, I told everyone I knew. I called friends I had not spoken to in months, goading them into asking the question, "What's new?"

I cannot tell you how much joy I got from offering an answer that began, "You will never guess who I met…"

I gave MJ a lot of honor (Is it obvious?), but… Michael does not call me. He has not sent me a text. He has not "friended" me on Facebook.

Does that mean I should not give him honor? No, but it does make me think about what motivates me to honor someone. And it makes me think about the people I *should* be honoring. What about the person who lives with me? The woman who looks to me for support, love and encouragement?

Why is it that we so easily give honor to celebrities, but withhold it from those we love the most? Why do we show more kindness and consideration to someone we have only known for five minutes than the person we are going to spend the rest of our lives with?

There are lots of reasons for this. For one, it is easy to overlook a person's imperfections when we do not live with that person twenty-four seven. It is easy to show honor when we do not have any reason to withhold it.

However, there is another reason – one that we fall prey to far too easily. We stereotype our spouse and say or think things like:

> *Men are always more logical.*
> *Women are always more emotional.*
> *Men are always thinking about sex.*

Okay, that last one might be true, but the other two? Nope. That word "always" makes them absolutely wrong. Stereotyping diminishes people and shoves them into a box marked "generic." However, when we see our spouses as they truly are, we magnify them. By embracing our spouse's uniqueness, we honor them; we fill up their soul.

We all know how a bicycle works, right? Pushing one pedal down brings the other up. Pushing that one down continues the cycle. This action gives the bike momentum.

Yes, it is metaphor time. Imagine for a moment that one pedal is love and the other is respect. When a husband presses the love pedal, it inspires his wife to press the respect pedal in return. Likewise, when the wife presses the respect pedal, the husband responds by pressing the love pedal. This works beautifully, moving a marriage forward in harmony – until someone gets hurt, disappointed or offended. Then someone stops pedaling.

> *"You disrespected me so I am going to stop treating you with love and kindness."*
> *"I do not feel loved so I will not show you respect."*

The relationship loses momentum. Honor disappears. The marriage stalls.

The Grass is Always Greener Where...

You are probably familiar with that old saying, "The grass is always greener on the other side of the fence." The message in that saying is pretty clear: you often see others' circumstances as better than your own. This usually happens when someone stops pedaling; when you feel devalued. It is a pretty depressing saying when you get right down to it.

I would like to suggest a more positive spin: "The grass is always green where you water it." Do you see how this is actually an answer to the former saying?

Relationships thrive when cultivated with honor, and thriving relationships keep you from coveting someone else's circumstance.

Early in our marriage, Holly called me out on my cultivation skills. I thought I was being a good, caring husband, but she told me I was merely "tolerating" her. She was right. Honor is not about tolerance – it is about intentionally loving and respecting your spouse.

Need another reason to honor your spouse? Here is a big one: Honor is the platform for intimacy and passion in a relationship. I think that is all I need to say about that.

Today, focus on what is important to your spouse. Say something that honors who they are.

And do not stop pedaling.

Takeaways

List three things that stood out to you in this chapter:

1.
2.
3.

Prayer

Pray this prayer before taking the next step:

"God, I want to have a marriage that is filled with honor. I want to genuinely honor my spouse and I want to feel honored. I invite the Holy Spirit to help create a home with an honoring environment. Lead me today. Show me what I need to do."

Actions

What specific things will you do today to work on honoring your spouse?

- _____
- _____
- _____

Day Three:
Admiration

Admiration and familiarity are strangers.
– George Sand

Admiration is our polite recognition of another's resemblance to ourselves.
– Ambrose Bierce

—✺—

Imagine a ladder. It is not a very tall ladder – just five rungs – but it can transform a relationship.

Let's call it, "The Admiration Ladder." This is what it looks like:

Admiration

Endorsement

Acceptance

Tolerance

Rejection

Remember what I admitted just a chapter ago? Holly had called me out – told me I was merely tolerating her instead of showing honor. That was more than a slap in the face, it was a wake-up call. On "The Admiration Ladder," tolerance is just one step up from rejection so I had a long way to go.

You might think rejection does not happen that often in relationship. Surely most people are better than that, right?

Have you ever said or thought any of these statements?

I wish you were different.

I wish you would change.

I wish you were more like me.

I wish you were more like my old boyfriend/ girlfriend.

These are words of rejection. They are words that plainly state, "I do not want you. I want someone else."

Ouch. This may be closer to home than you want to admit. Have you said any of these things? This might be a good time to ask forgiveness for your words. Forgiveness will be discussed further in an upcoming chapter, but you know the basics, so do not delay.

Are you guilty of spending time on the rejection rung? You cannot stay here long, because a relationship quickly becomes untenable if you linger. However, there are only two directions to go.

How about taking a step up?

Ah, tolerance. This rung has a familiar ring to it, doesn't it? We do a lot of tolerating in our daily lives; we are experts at it. We tolerate the friend who cannot stop talking about her perfect children; the neighbor who always parks his truck in front of our house; the co-worker who bathes in perfume and sits upwind and we tolerate our spouses. Tolerance is not quite as ugly as rejection, but it smells almost as bad as that over-perfumed co-worker.

Tolerance says, "I don't like what you are doing, but I'm going to endure it because I'm such a kind-hearted person." Tolerance, like rejection, is not selfless at all. It is all about us. We think we are being generous when we are tolerant. We want "points" for being tolerant. Sorry. No points awarded here.

While relationships cannot stay on the rejection rung for long before something has to change, far too many couples languish for years in the tolerance zone. Do not get stuck here. Look up and climb another rung…to acceptance.

Most marriages live and die on the acceptance rung. Think about it; if we can learn to accept each other we will survive, maybe even for a lifetime. But, is survival what we want in our marriage? Sure, we all go through survival seasons, but when we find ourselves there our goal should be to climb higher on the ladder.

Love demands that we climb.

When we climb from acceptance, we find ourselves at endorsement. This is a great place to be in relationship. It is more than mere acceptance of your spouse; it is honoring their uniqueness.

Picture yourself in a conversation with a friend. Acceptance answers the question, "How is your marriage?" with, "Fine, we are just fine." Endorsement answers it with specific, honoring truths like, "My wife is an amazing writer," or, "My husband is so good with the kids." Endorsement comes from knowing your spouse well, and it is fueled by joy.

If you think the endorsement rung is great, wait until you reach for admiration. While intention and strength help you climb the ladder, it is actually humility that allows you to reach the top rung. Admiration is what jealousy wishes it were. It is the place where you not only acknowledge your spouse's unique gifts, you are humbled by them and how they make your marriage better.

Admiration is the place where relationships go to truly thrive.

> *Be devoted to one another in love. Honor one another above yourselves.*
> (Romans 12:10)

Over the next few days, focus on "The Admiration Ladder" and see if you can move up a rung or two. Your marriage will flourish.

Now before we move on to **Day Four**, I think we need to talk a bit about the differences between a husband and wife. Yes, some of these are rather obvious, but it is worth a refresher course here. Misunderstanding these differences makes it difficult to climb "The Admiration Ladder."

Recognize and Admire Your Differences

We make a great leap in maturity when we realize we have differences because God made us that way – not because one of us is flawed and the other is not. In my marriage, this issue almost buried us. (P.S. *It is an ongoing issue.*)

We have differences because of personality. Maybe you are an extrovert and your spouse is an introvert. Perhaps one person is people-oriented and the other is project-oriented. One may be detailed and the other visionary. Guess what? One is not better than the other.

We have differences because of our backgrounds or upbringing. My wife comes from a wealthy, nurturing family. She had lived in several countries before she was sixteen years old. I mean exotic places like Indonesia, Venezuela, England and...well...Philadelphia. By contrast, the first time I ever left the States was when I went on a mission trip – *at thirty years of age.* Holly was given great opportunities and they came easily for her. I had to work really hard for every little success. She had a great education and is really intelligent. On the other hand, I probably do not need to belabor the point.

We have differences because of our strengths and weaknesses. This may seem rather obvious, but it is important to say it "out loud." By the way, many weaknesses are just a strength - taken too far. Kind of changes your perspective a bit, doesn't it?

We have differences because of gender. Men and women are just different. This goes beyond the plumbing. (Of course you have to love the plumbing.) Women want to know and feel that they are loved and they are important. This is crucial. Men want to know that you respect who they are and what they do.

Some of the most contentious issues in a marriage are born of gender differences. We will explore how this plays out in communication in the Connection chapter, but I do want to offer one main thought here: Wives, here is all you really need to know about your husband: He is simple. He is not stupid, he is not insensitive – he is just simpler than you are. This affects the way he communicates, the way he responds to crisis and just about everything else in life.

It is also important to note that some of our gender-spawned differences are not as stark as we think they are. Take movies, for example. Women usually enjoy movies about relationships. They get all excited about *It's Complicated, He's Just Not That Into You, Four Weddings and a Funeral,* or *Water for Elephants*. They cannot get enough of *Sleepless in Seattle* or *The Notebook*. Guys tend to roll their eyes at these sorts of films. Oh, your husband will go, but mostly because he loves you and wants to show you honor, not because he is looking forward to the weepy scene where the guy races to the airport to admit he has been a fool and that he is really in love with the girl after all.

I am going to let you in on a little secret: men like relationship movies too. Their relationship movies just go by different names, like *The Bourne Identity, Limitless, Remember the Titans, Iron Man,* and *Braveheart*.

For men, movie relationships are all about camaraderie and teamwork in accomplishing a specific goal (being victorious in battle, winning the big game, solving a puzzle). For women, it is all about the chase – the relationship dance itself – and their goals are usually more about love than explosions. The truth is both husbands and wives long for relationship – they just see it differently.

Let's take a look at how differences can lead to rejection or tolerance instead of endorsement and admiration. I think both husbands and wives will relate to this one. I call it "The Five-Minute Dilemma."

It takes me ten minutes to get ready to go somewhere, unless I have to shower, too. Then it takes twelve. Holly needs a little more time. This is where it all starts.

Like most men, my communication style is literal and specific (we will talk more about that later). Holly tends to be more metaphorical or symbolic.

"Holly, are you ready to go?"

"Yes, I am ready," she says.

Despite years of evidence to the contrary, I am thinking this means "I am ready right now," so I go out and start the car. However, when she says, "I am ready," what she really means is, "I am approaching a state of readiness. I will be landing there soon, depending on prevailing winds."

And that space between my "ready" and hers? It is just waiting for an argument. Patience and understanding would keep that argument at bay, but men are not always good at either.

So I say in frustration, "You said five minutes."

"That was seven minutes ago."

Holly is ready for my complaint. (And here lies more evidence of her intelligence.) "When I said five minutes, I meant like the five minutes that you tell me are left in the basketball game on TV," she says.

Cue awkward silence.
"Oh. Got it. "

Sometimes, the *similarities* in past experiences can make it difficult for us to climb "The Admiration Ladder." Bonnie and Anthony faced that in their marriage so I will let Bonnie tell her story here:

> Neither my husband nor I grew up with the best father figures. My father was verbally and psychologically abusive to my mother and me and ruled us with an iron fist. We did as he said and always made sure family and friends thought we were the happiest family around. We lived in a pretend world and never discussed what we really felt.
>
> As a little girl I internalized so much, developed eating disorders, and was having panic attacks by ten years old. I never really knew what I truly did feel because I wasn't allowed to talk about it. I carried these hurts with me into my marriage.
>
> It wasn't much easier for my husband. His father raised him with the kind of tough love that included far too many hurtful words. He felt disconnected, un-admired and that he was a disappointment.
>
> We were a recipe for marriage disaster, and we did have our struggles, but I remember watching my husband play with our 3-year old triplets. He just lit up playing with the girls. They covered him in kisses and trusted

him fully as he lavished them with words of affirmation, love, admiration, honor, respect, hope, and faith.

I should have been happy watching this, and I was, but all I could do was cry. I cried sad tears for the little girl inside of me who missed out on this...but they were also tears of joy because my little girls would not have to experience what I did! In that moment, I felt true admiration for my husband.

My husband had found a way to rebuild a bridge in both of our hearts by making the decision to be the husband and father God created him to be. He broke generational curses and stood in the gap for our family. By understanding each other's stories, and taking steps to overcome the challenges we knew were there, we were both able to discover levels of admiration for one another that could not have been achieved otherwise.

Bonnie and Anthony could have become another divorce statistic if they had not considered their upbringing and found a way to work through those tricky issues together. Instead, they found that path, with God's help, and climbed the ladder to true admiration.

Today, begin to demonstrate acceptance of your spouse. Then keep working on it. Love doesn't stop there. Make it your goal to reach the rung of admiration. And do not be shy telling your spouse about that admiration.

Takeaways

List three things that stood out to you in this chapter:

1.
2.
3.

Prayer

Pray this prayer before taking the next step:

"If I have communicated little more than tolerance to my spouse, show me how to change that. Teach me how to express acceptance, endorsement and admiration. Lord, help me to show honor in a way that causes my spouse to feel that honor sincerely and soul-deep."

Actions

What specific things will you do today to work on admiration in your marriage?

* _____
* _____
* _____

Day Four:
Trust

The best way to find out if you can trust somebody is to trust them.
– Ernest Hemingway

Above all else, guard your heart... for everything flows from it.
(Proverbs 4:23)

What's scarce in the world is...attention and trust.
– Seth Godin

——《◇》——

J eff said all the right things. Diane heard what every wife wants to hear:

When I look at you I see the ultimate woman.
No other woman will ever capture my heart.
The search for the woman of my dreams
ended when I met you.

One day, after five years of marriage, Diane found a strange note in the pocket of his jeans. The note led her to his computer. The computer led her to his cell phone messages. And the cell phone messages led her to doubt everything he had ever said.

Ultimate woman? Ultimate fool, more likely.
How many other women have pieces of his heart?
Apparently the search is not over after all.

"Lies. All his words had been lies," she thought. "He broke my heart. How can I ever trust him again?" she said. It might as well have been a rhetorical question.

Carl and I were talking over coffee one day. He turned suddenly serious and said, "My wife told our friends about some of our personal issues. I was so embarrassed. She betrayed me. Who else has she shared our business with? What else has she revealed to others? I thought marriage was about supporting each other!"

Diane and Carl are both victims of a far-too-common marriage malady: *broken trust*. This is no small thing. Trust is the glue that makes relationships work. Trust, built over time, is what makes a relationship strong, and yet there is a paradox here because trust can be snapped in an instant.

No one loves Holly more than I do, but loving her does not mean I cannot hurt her. Because I know her better than anyone, I have hurt her more than anyone. No one loves me more than Holly does and because she knows how to push my buttons, no one has hurt me more.

When we love someone, we place value on the things they say and do. This gives them a rare power over us that can be used for good or evil. When a spouse encourages and uplifts us, we feel like we can fly, but when they say or do something that hurts, we feel it like a punch to the stomach. There is nothing as sharp as the shards of broken trust.

Such is the nature of trust. Trust means giving someone permission to heal and to hurt. You cannot have one without the other. Risk is *inherent* in trust.

> *We're never so vulnerable than when we trust someone – but paradoxically, if we cannot trust, neither can we find love or joy.*
> – Walter Anderson

Because of this and because we are human, it is unrealistic to believe that trust will never be broken, even in the best of relationships. This does not mean we offer license to hurt one another. It also does not mean we can excuse our behavior simply by claiming our humanness. Saying, "I am only human," is a cop out. Doing so is blaming our error on the human condition instead of accepting specific responsibility for our specific actions. Before we can rebuild trust, we have to accept responsibility for breaking it.

Trust is something we earn. And yet, as the Hemingway quote above says, "The best way to find out if you can trust someone is to trust them." Does this seem like a contradiction?

It is not. The first statement speaks to the person who hopes to be trusted. We do not deserve to be trusted; we have to earn it by being trustworthy. Hemingway's statement is directed to the person who is being asked to trust. We can only know if someone is trustworthy by granting them that gift.

When Trust is Broken

So what happens when we do something that breaks that trust?

Well, the first thing to do is to admit our error, to ask for forgiveness, and then to commit to "whatever it takes" to earn it back. Humility is the starting place for regaining trust. Honesty is the currency that buys it back over time.

Did you see those two words, "over time"? They are so critical to building trust. Both parties can become impatient with the time it takes to rebuild trust. The guilty party may feel stymied at first, wondering if his wife will ever stop looking at him with that "evil eye of distrust." Even though he had earned it with his actions, he wants to change – he has changed, but she is not ready to trust yet.

It is important to recognize that in a very real way, you have to *earn* it back. One of the greatest ways to earn trust is to start showing some results. If you say you are going to change, then start changing. If you say you are going to meet needs, listen more or be loyal, nothing is more convincing than progress in those areas. Fruit is the reason to trust.

It is hard to trust promises alone if the past is defined by broken promises.

A cocaine addict who has lied and manipulated for years can gain trust by getting help, following through and being accountable to a sponsor or mentor. Fruit is gained little by little, first by being clean for a week, then a month, then several months and then years.

Momentum is a trust-builder's friend.

Jesus said, "You will know them by their fruit." He warns us not to think we can get the kind of fruit we are hoping for from a tree that does not produce that kind of fruit. Be willing to show your spouse the kind of fruit that is needed to rebuild trust.

What about the person who was damaged by trust? Well, she is often just as impatient with the process, too. She wishes she could just flip a switch and turn trust on full blast, but she cannot. It takes time to sort through the pain, and she is not ready to risk being hurt again. Not yet.

If you are the one trying to learn how to trust again, it is important to recognize that you might have "trust issues" too. Did you have trouble trusting before your marriage? Do you have trouble trusting men, women, leaders, family or those whom you get close to?

Before I married Holly I knew only one familiar pattern: *The people I cared about would argue, then yell, then ultimately leave.* It happened in relationships with my parents, with family, friends and previous girlfriends. So when Holly and I had our first argument (and our 101st), I panicked. "That is it," I thought, "She is going to leave." It did not seem right in my head, but my heart only knew one pattern of behavior.

Holly did not leave. She stayed. She stayed some more and she loved me. It was her love and her persistence that helped me heal and trust. Now when we have heated discussions, there is no trigger going off inside that keeps me from trusting her.

One way I learned to build trust in our relationship was how I responded to her when she came to me with a frustration. In the past, when she would come to me and say, "I do not feel like I am important to you," I would answer, "What are you talking about? Of course I think you are important. You are just being emotional. I have told you 'I love you' a thousand times."

This was not the right thing to say. By challenging her (or more accurately, not really listening), I had become an unsafe place for her to talk about feelings. We need to be a safe place for our spouse to share or trust simply cannot grow.

Now if my wife comes to me and says, "Philip, I do not feel like you love me. I feel like everything else is more important to you," I say something like, "I'm sorry for anything I have said or done that would cause you to feel that way. I don't want you to ever feel that way because of something I have done. I will do anything I can to make sure I never make you feel that way again. Help me know how to do that."

This leads to a *totally* different conversation.

Before you can truly grow trust, you must let your spouse know that you are safe, that she can talk to you and trust you with feelings, no matter how harsh or painful they might at first appear. You need to let your spouse know that you are not going to attack her, put her down or get defensive.

Showing someone that *you are* willing to trust can encourage them to trust you back.

Recently, a friend shared a powerful story with me that illustrates many of the challenging aspects of trust. She wished to remain anonymous, so I have honored that here. In a way that anonymity is appropriate because there are so many other women who have quietly endured the very same sort of experience. Perhaps this story will help some of them realize they are not alone and that there is hope for rebuilding trust.

To be honest, I think I just assumed every husband on Earth cheats on his wife and/or has a porn addiction. I grew up in a home where both were present. It never made sense to me. My mother is beautiful. She is bright, funny, and extremely capable. She is a great cook and to this day, has a great career – she loves her family, loves people. Why would anyone cheat on her?

Growing up, I watched my parents wrestle in what I now know was a co-dependent relationship. My father was an emotionally abusive, absent taker and my mom worked overtime, not only to cover it up, but to make up for it.

I marveled at her strength and her beauty and she instilled in me a strong work ethic, good morals and a passion for people. At the same time I adopted her tendency to bury feelings.

The most devastating character defect I learned from my father was silence. Silence was the most lethal form of control in our home. He used this tactic on my mother to avoid conflict or to coerce her into doing what he was actually responsible for.

When I first learned of my father's affairs, I remember crying and then burying it somewhere deep inside – we did not talk about those kinds of things in our family and under no circumstances would we have shared that with a trusted friend or teacher or counselor.

As I became a teenager and then a college student, I continued to watch young boys and young men cheat on their girlfriends and treat women wrongly. Even though I had grown up with both parents in my home, I still had a deep-rooted longing for connection and in many ways, had the heart of an orphan. I believe I was aching for my father's love and endorsement. When I could not find that validation in a healthy place, I began to party hard using drugs and alcohol, and I developed an eating disorder, bulimia.

Then one weekend in college, a guy I knew on campus raped me. I did not tell anyone. I woke up and went to work the next morning like nothing had happened. A series of unhealthy relationships followed and during one of the longer relationships, I decided to move to Los Angeles.

Two weeks before I moved, I discovered I was pregnant. I was devastated. I made the decision that night to have an abortion. I did not even want to tell my boyfriend, but when I did, he did not try to stop me.

In my heart, I truly believed that men could not be trusted. They were not worthy of admiration or forgiveness. I believed they were all unfaithful and emotionally unavailable. At a core level, I think I believed this about God, too.

I moved to Los Angeles with all that pain and brokenness. I was literally sick with secrets from my past. Then I met some male co-workers at my first job in Los Angeles and they were the first men in years who did not try to sleep with me and who did not seem to care about what I looked like. I was more than an object. I felt like a sister – someone they looked out for.

I ended up coming to church with them and experienced radical healing and transformation. That is when I met Philip and Holly. God used them to teach me that my feelings matter and there is a healthy way to express them. I learned that forgiving my dad, my rapist, and all the men in my past actually set me free.

Eight years later, I met my husband. He has a past too, but has experienced the life-changing power of Jesus and the transformation that the local church community offers us. We understand that our differences make us stronger and if we learn to love and respect each other, we will create a marriage that expresses honor. We know how to say we are sorry – we know how to listen to advice and the counsel of our pastors and leaders. We ask for help when we need it (and sometimes before).

> Because of my background, sometimes I struggle to open up to my husband or I am afraid to share my true feelings. Sometimes a familiar silence creeps its way into our home, but my husband is patient, honoring and kind. He asks questions; he sits with me and lets me know that when I am ready to talk he wants to hear. He is not angry about my background – he is gracious with me and I understand the love of my Father in heaven more clearly because of who my husband is. I am learning not to control with silence or to be controlled by silence. Just because we were raised a certain way does not mean we have to live that way.

Do you see that last sentence? Read it again. It is so important and so true.

We all have baggage; some of it makes the very idea of trust seem like an impossible dream. However, with time, patience, wise counsel and God's help, we can learn to trust. Time is not the enemy of trust – it is the friend.

I need to add here that if you or your spouse has a past marked by sexual abuse, it may take extra time and compassion to work through those deep-rooted trust issues. You may need some professional help. A licensed Christian marriage and family counselor can be a valuable investment in this area.

Meanwhile, wherever you are in your journey of trust, it might be a good idea to shore up your forgiveness skills. That is the topic for **Day Five**.

Few things can help an individual more than to place responsibility on him, and to let him know that you trust him.
– Booker T. Washington

You may be deceived if you trust too much, but you will live in torment if you do not trust enough.
– Frank Crane

Takeaways

List three things that stood out to you in this chapter:

1.
2.
3.

Prayer

Pray this prayer before taking the next step:
"Lord, help us to trust each other. Show me what I need to do to earn trust at a deeper level. Help me see when I am being unreasonable and not giving trust when it is deserved. Show me how to be a spouse who is 'safe' to talk to and can be counted on for love and strength."

Actions

What specific things will you do today to work on trust?

- _____
- _____
- _____

Day Five:
Forgiveness

Always forgive your enemies – nothing annoys them so much.
– Oscar Wilde

And forgive us our debts, as we also have forgiven our debtors.
(Matthew 6:12)

Next time I see you, remind me not to talk to you.
– Groucho Marx

—∿∿∿—

A few years ago a gunman walked into an Amish schoolroom and murdered several little children and then killed himself. The story was all over the news. How could someone do such a horrific thing? How would the families ever get over this tragedy?

The next day, in an amazing display of forgiveness, the Amish leaders went to the home of the murderer's widowed wife and told her that they forgave her husband and wanted to offer help in her time of pain.

What an incredible gesture of grace. It spoke highly about the values of the Amish community and turned the attention of the world from pondering tragedy to pondering forgiveness, but I suspect some who heard about this grand act of grace thought the Amish leaders foolish. Where was their righteous (and certainly well-deserved) anger? Where was the outrage?

Forgiveness had banished anger and outrage, replacing both of them with love.

There is, however, another layer to this story. At the time of this event, the Amish community was practicing shunning: The act of excommunicating or rejecting members who broke certain established rules or codes, such as not dressing properly or befriending people outside the community.

What a contrast. On the one hand, we observe a most amazing expression of forgiveness and on the other we see rejection for such relatively minor offenses.

Is this selective mercy?

We often do this in our relationships. We believe in a message of grace and forgiveness and we happily declare it to strangers we are trying to "love into" our faith. Grand gestures of forgiveness make us feel good about our God and about ourselves, but the shortcomings of our spouses are somehow unforgiveable?

Sarah-Gayle knows first-hand about this challenge. Her story reveals another truth about the obstacles to forgiveness. This is her story:

> When Chad and I first got married, I had an extremely difficult time saying that I was sorry. I refused because it would mean admitting that I actually did something wrong. Growing up, doing something wrong meant disapproving, degrading, discouraging words from my father.
>
> Additionally, when Chad would say "Sorry" to me for something he had done, it did not mean anything to me. I held grudges for days and shut down on him. I always thought his words were insincere.
>
> I was awakened to my need to change by two events. First, I noticed in the fourth year of

our marriage that our two-year-old son would not say "Sorry" for his bad behavior. Though it should have been obvious, considering my past, I was blind to the reason. One day I was sitting in my room, feeling horrible because my husband was upset with me about some-thing, but I was not willing to apologize. Then it clicked – I understood what was going on with my son. That was a rude awakening.

The second event occurred when I was work-ing toward my master's degree in marriage and family therapy. One of the requirements was forty hours of personal therapy. I thought it would be fun to bring my husband along. We could have some laughs and look into each other's eyes and talk about our amazing relationship, but it was not quite so delightful as that. This is how the conversation went:

Therapist: "So when your feelings are hurt and you feel that Chad is to blame, 'Sorry' from him doesn't quite cut it does it?"

Me: "No, not at all. He says it too quickly and I cannot believe that he is sorry."

Therapist: "He needs to sweat a little right? He needs to truly understand that he cannot hurt you that way and that he needs to win back your affection. He needs to truly show you that he is sorry, maybe even more than once."

Me: "Oh my gosh, yes!" [*Finally*, I thought, *someone who gets me!*]

Therapist: "No."

Me: [Or not.] "No?"

Therapist: "When you get hurt, you are asking your husband to not only apologize and 'pay for' what happened between the two of you, but also what happened in your upbringing. That is why your response is so extreme. You have anger rooted to your upbringing, where you experienced the lack of freedom to have your own voice. This anger lashes out when someone hurts you. If the anger could talk it would say, 'Make them pay, I cannot believe they did that to you. Now take control of those hurt feelings you feel and have felt over the years and hold a grudge.'"

This was a life changing moment for me. I realized that my inability to apologize or accept apologies was costing me authentic love, and that not only was I setting my son up to repeat the same cycle, I was training my husband to walk on egg shells.

When I saw the cost, I knew I had to change. God had so much more for my family and me. I began to see that the life I wanted to live, a life honoring God with everything, was not congruent to the life that I was living.

It was an excruciating process as I failed time and time again, but the more I learned to trust God's help, the less painful it became to apologize and truly forgive. I finally felt free. I did not have to be perfect and neither did those around me. And I am happy to say that my son began to say "Sorry" too.

Forgiveness is the highest expression of God's love. When Jesus taught his followers to pray, "Forgive us our debts as we forgive our debtors," he was not just sharing prayer tips, he was establishing the foundation of his message.

From a purely theological point of view, forgiveness allows a relationship to continue. Without forgiveness, we remain far from God. The same is true in our human-to-human relationships, without forgiveness we grow distant from one another. Forgiveness gives relationships the opportunity to continue, and more than that, to thrive.

> *It is easier to forgive an enemy than to forgive a friend.*
> – William Blake

The Power of Forgiveness

Why is it so easy to forgive strangers and not our spouses? Proximity, mostly. We do not live with those strangers. We do not notice how they always leave hair in the sink or the toilet seat up or empty milk cartons in the fridge. From a distance, forgiveness is (usually) easy, but up close it is difficult. We would rather hold an offense against our spouses than forgive because doing so gives us a sense of power.

It is not real power. It is selfishness masquerading as power.

Forgiveness is where the real power is and it is a freeing power. We need to tear up the IOUs we are hoarding. (Or would that be UOMs? After all, withholding forgiveness is usually all about what "you owe me.")

Peter brought up this topic of forgiveness to Jesus in front of the other disciples once.

"Jesus, I've got a question for you," he says. (This is the Philip Wagner version.) "Imagine this scenario. Let's say that someone offends me. Maybe they say something about my mother or they make some comment about how I speak before I think. I am kind of making this up as I go along here, Lord. So, what should my response be?" Peter asks.

Jesus knows that Peter is flexing his spiritual mercy muscles and wanting to display how much he has grown in this 'love stuff,' but he invites him to continue.

"Forgive them, what about seven times? Because, I can do that. I can totally do seven. You know in the Law of Moses I think it is like an eye for an eye or something, but I think I am ready to forgive...wait for it... seven times."

Jesus' answer is not what Peter is expecting. "Not seven times, Peter," he says. "Seventy times seven."

Jesus has a higher standard for us in almost every area.

Jesus is so clear that forgiveness is the core expression of our faith that he does not stop there. He goes on to suggest that we love our enemies; but let's take one step at a time here.

We need to learn how to forgive for the petty things, the disappointments, the frustrations and the expectations that pile up. Sometimes we also have to forgive big things. Yes, I am talking about betrayal, addictive behaviors, even unfaithfulness.

Forgiveness and Adultery

Let's look at the Big One in that list: *Adultery*. It is true that the Bible allows for a believer to get a divorce if a spouse commits adultery, but I do not think this path is the highest expression of God's love. The Bible also allows for forgiveness and the miracle of new and greater love. Is that not the Gospel story in a nutshell?

I am not suggesting that husbands or wives subject themselves to abuse of any kind, but many salvageable marriages end because one or both parties see divorce as the only possible solution. They wield the D-word as a threat until they have dashed all hope of reconciliation. When a married couple goes through this kind of crisis, the marriage seems doomed.

However, it does not have to be.

Forgiveness for big offenses is difficult, disappointing, and sometimes disillusioning. Rebuilding a marriage after it has been broken is like trying to piece together a shattered vase. Nevertheless, there is healing, trust can be rebuilt, and couples who find their way through forgiveness often come away with a deeper, more intimate, and amazingly fulfilling relationship. It takes time, it takes work, it takes patience and sometimes it may seem impossible, but it is worth the effort.

I want to ask you, as a believer, to consider the power and grace of forgiveness. I am not asking you to risk your life or subject yourself to harm or abuse, but if your spouse has messed up and you truly want to make it right, your faith asks you to forgive. You are a forgiven person, so it should be within you to forgive.

Are you holding offenses against your spouse? Are you shunning him or her?

In Ephesians 4:32, the Apostle Paul tells us to "be kind and compassionate to one another, forgiving each other, just as in Christ God forgave you."

A healthy, thriving marriage is made up of two people who know how to forgive one another.

Check for a root of bitterness in your relationship. Then, with God's help, let go of the past.

We are not as skilled as God is in the "forget" part of "forgive and forget," but with God's help we can stop looking backward. And we sure need to stop looking backward if we want to move our relationship forward.

Make certain your windshield is bigger than your rear view mirror and determine to have a debt-free relationship.

It is **Day Five**. Today you may need to forgive your spouse. Do that. You may have to forgive someone several times in your heart before the pain of a single offense will fade. Commit to that path. Decide today that you will live a lifestyle of forgiveness.

Now you know what it is like to forgive. It is a good feeling, isn't it? Well, get used to forgiving. You will probably have to do it again sometime.

We all still have a long way to go before we are perfect.

Takeaways

List three things that stood out to you in this chapter:

1.
2.
3.

Prayer

Pray this prayer before taking the next step:

"Lord, I am making the decision today to forgive my spouse. I am going to forgive for the little things and the big things. I do not think this will always be easy, so I need your help. Show me how to live by the law of love and forgiveness. I want to forgive others the way you have forgiven me. Give me your grace to love like you love."

Actions

What specific things will you do today to work on forgiveness?

- _____
- _____
- _____

Day Six:
Change

Women marry men hoping they will change. Men marry women hoping they will not.
– Albert Einstein

Change is such hard work.
– Billy Crystal

Let God transform you into a new person by changing the way you think. Then you will learn to know God's will for you, which is good and pleasing and perfect.
– Apostle Paul

I have ADD. This makes me unpredictable, mysterious, spontaneous and just this side of genius.

Are you buying any of this?

Here is a familiar conversation:

> Holly: "Where is your wallet?"
> Me: "What makes you think I don't have it?"
> Holly: "Where is your wallet?"
> Me: "I know where my keys are."
> Holly: "Where is your wallet?"
> Me: "Just give it to me. I didn't know I lost it."
> Holly: "I found it. In the hallway. On the floor. Why can't you just put it in the same place? Every time. How can you keep losing your things?"
> Me: "Holly, I am sorry. Really. You don't know how hard I try."
> Holly: "So where *are* your keys?"
> Me: "Somewhere…in California. Kidding! They are right here in my pocket."

I pat my front pants pocket only to realize the pocket is empty.

Great. She noticed. She knows.

I have tried to change. I really have. Apparently there are some things we can change and others we cannot, but dedication to growth as a person, a spouse or a Christian is essential. A personal dedication to growth makes all the difference in the world.

What do you want people to say about you when you are not in the room? What are you doing to deserve that?

You have probably heard the saying, "the only constant in life is change." I think science fiction author Isaac Asimov might have said it first, but there is nothing "fiction" about it. Change is inevitable. The world is changing faster than many of us can keep up. Remember rotary dial phones? You don't? Er...right...neither do I. Apparently phones used to be tethered to the wall, too. Hard to believe, isn't it.

While change in the world around us is inevitable change within is not. Some have said it takes twenty-one days to form or change a habit. I think for some of us, it is more like twenty-one weeks. Billy Crystal is right, "Change is...hard work."

Nevertheless, change we must. Especially if the things we are currently doing hurt the people we care about. In order to take a marriage to new heights of happiness, contentment, joy and intimacy, we often have to change beliefs, actions and attitudes.

When I say "we" I mean you. Or me. Despite our persistence and insistence to prove this wrong, we cannot change someone else. We can only change ourselves.

This is why I am quick to encourage those who are still single and searching for love to look for someone who is dedicated to personal growth, humble, quick to admit wrongs, and quick to accept responsibility for his or her actions. This kind of person is a keeper – just the sort of person who will also naturally pursue change in the future whenever beliefs, actions or attitudes are not what they should be.

Now let me double click on this for a minute. First, some wise words from a brilliant man:

> *The problems we face today cannot be solved from the same level of thinking that created them.*
> – Albert Einstein

In other words, what got you here is not going to get you where you want to go.

If you want to have a great marriage, you have to put extra effort into growing. Why? Because over time you get stale. You start to cruise, passion wanes. You face a new problem and are not equipped with the answer.

The answer to that problem, the miracle you need, could come from just a little more information. Information you might find at a marriage seminar, or in a book on communication, or on a podcast about enhancing your relationship. Great advice, new ideas and a heart-to-heart conversation could be the difference between a marriage that is heaven on earth and one that is a living hell.

In order to be great husbands and wives, we need a teachable spirit.

If you are married to someone who refuses to change or is far from having a teachable spirit, you may ask, "What am I supposed to do?" The only thing you can do is focus on the changes *you* need to make. When you try to force change in someone else, you become controlling, and no one likes to feel controlled.

Controlling behaviors drive most people away. People will want to change only when they recognize the benefit of that change, not when someone else tells them they have to.

An important note: If your spouse's behaviors are abusive or dangerous and there is little hope of positive change, you may need to make difficult, yet critical, decisions to protect yourself.

Some people say it took Edison ten-thousand tries and failures before he invented the electric light. I have also heard it was more like two-thousand failed attempts. Personally, I do not want to try and fail one-hundred times at something, let alone two-thousand or ten-thousand. Whatever number is true, the message in Edison's story is clear: Do not give up until you figure it out. And you know what else?

Change takes work.

Take your sex life for instance. (Okay, maybe there is one area where I would not mind trying two-thousand times without getting it exactly right.) So many loving couples struggle with their sex lives. One spouse loses the passion, the other gets frustrated. If you are suffering from this issue, or even if you just want to take your sex life to a "whole 'notha level," you have to do some work. You may need to work on your attitude and your actions, you may need to invest time, ask questions, listen and adjust your approach. It could be that you have a lot to learn about pleasing your spouse. It could be that after a few years your spouse's preference or interests have changed.

Whatever the problem is, it is worth the effort to solve things and to change as needed so you can find the passion again.

One of the most common areas where we need to change is overcoming past hurts.

The basis for how we respond to most situations and people is rooted in our subconscious. Each of our unique personal histories is like a field, and it is littered with land mines – baggage from previous relationships or circumstances or choices made or unmade. And these mines can be unintentionally (or intentionally) triggered by as little as a word or look from our spouse.

We all have past hurts. Resolving those hurts and dealing with contentious baggage is crucial to a healthy, happy, intimacy-filled marriage.

Alex and Shunna were on the road to divorce and the end was near. They had lived together for five years and only been married for two, but the relationship was falling apart fast. Like so many others, they turned to God as a final resort – one last chance to save a failing marriage, which He did. He showed them what a picture of a healthy, thriving marriage based on unconditional love and respect looked like. The path to that discovery was a difficult one that began long before they even knew each other.

Shunna's father had abandoned her and her mother. Her stepdad had been physically and emotionally abusive. It was not until years later that she realized her expectations for her own marriage had been negatively shaped by these experiences.

> "I was always waiting for the bomb to drop and for it all to explode," she says. "Deep inside I knew this marriage thing probably would not work. Little did I know, I was the one making my low expectations a reality. I had not yet realized that with God's help I could turn things around; that I could deal with all the baggage."

Alex had no real example of a father or a husband in his life. His story is a little like Shunna's: his father abandoned their family when he was a small boy.

When things got difficult in their marriage, Alex and Shunna had to change. They had to learn how to see and believe the best in themselves and each other. They had to learn to "fight fair," to communicate honestly and with honor. They had to learn how to prefer one another and to put the other's need first.

It seems so simple, but when you learn that you are both on the same team and actually act that way, things do begin to change. You change, your spouse changes, your marriage changes.

Shunna and Alex first had to change their perspectives and expectations. They did not want to repeat the same poor choices their parents had made and they did not have to.

They decided to set a new standard for what marriage looked like in their family. They started fresh by renewing their vows to each other and to God. They took the "D" word out of their vocabulary – forever. They attended marriage conferences, joined small groups and went to workshops. They developed great friendships with other couples who were on a similar journey to discover a fun, fulfilling and healthy marriage.

They went through their share of trials and challenging issues, not always perfectly, but with grace and openness. They experienced the power of prayer and learned how they could be part of the answer to prayer.

It has been thirteen years since they began this process. It works!

Develop the Skill of *Getting Past Your Past*

I have come to believe that one of the great skills in life is the ability to get past our past, which may be the hardest changes any of us has to make. It takes work, time, forgiveness, and perhaps even professional counseling, but letting yesterday's sorrows go is like removing a lead-lined overcoat. We feel lighter, more agile, and more able to move toward the person we married.

I have a dog named Angel, a lab mix and she is a good, loyal and obedient dog. A few years ago she developed a large sore on her leg, which the vet told me was quite common. When a dog gets a small cut they lick it to help the healing, but some dogs lick and lick and lick and lick some more. They become fixated on the sore and make it worse. The sore gets red and swollen and becomes more of a problem than the original wound.

Angel was that kind of dog, so she was given one of those cones that wraps around the dog's neck to block her from licking the sore. She had to wear it for about a month. The wound healed, I took the cone off and that was that.

Until about six months later.

Then it happened all over again – the licking, the growing sore, the cone, the eventual healing. It has become an annual tradition. These days when I bring out the collar and call her over, Angel looks at the cone, offers a pleading look, then gives in, puts her head down and walks slowly toward me.

It is as if she is saying, "The cone of shame… again? What will all my friends say?"

I wonder if we had a cone for humans if it would keep us from fixating on our old wounds. Maybe we do have that cone. Perhaps that "cone" could be our spouse or a close friend or a counselor, someone who can speak the truth in love. Someone who can say, "I love you, I feel bad about what you went through, but I have heard it about – let's see twenty-three times now. It is time to let it go."

Letting go of the past is a positive step toward emotional health, which is important to a marriage. An emotionally healthy person is someone who can say these things, and mean them:

> *I am valuable,*
> *I have a great future.*
> *I am loved, I have friends who value and respect me.*

I have a mission that involves helping others.
The past is the past – the best is yet to come.

There are a variety of different paths to emotional health and each person has to discover the path that works best for him or her. Remember, we can only change ourselves, but here is a simple four-step process to get things rolling.

1. Face it.
Admit the hurts. Admit the wounds. Bringing your personal problems into the light is the first step toward bringing healing to your soul.

2. Ask God for help.
In Matthew 11:2 Jesus said, "Come to me, all you who are weary and burdened, and I will give you rest." Jesus told us that He has the power of the Holy Spirit to heal the broken-hearted. He is available. Nuff said.

3. Talk about your hurts with people who can be trusted.
This might be a close friend or professional counselor, but whomever you choose, make sure the person is both trustworthy and respectful of confidentiality. Note to husbands: You know that really nice woman you work with who is such a good listener? Do not choose her. Nope. And wives? Do not choose that kind-hearted neighbor guy who likes to chat over the fence. If you share your hurts with someone of the opposite sex (who is not a professional counselor), you are just asking for trouble.

4. Open your heart for healing.

Keeping up walls prevents you from being able to heal. Yes, there is risk in letting down the walls, but that is the only way you will find your way to emotional health. It is the only way you can become a more loving and compassionate person.

I am going to end this chapter with a real challenge. It is going to stretch you a bit and might make you a bit uncomfortable. (Change usually does.) Ready? Okay, here you go: *Love as if you have never been hurt before; trust like you have never been betrayed before.*

I know, but try it anyway.

Takeaways

List three things that stood out to you in this chapter:

1.
2.
3.

Prayer

Pray this prayer before taking the next step:

"Teach me your ways, Lord. Show me your paths. I need to grow as a person and as your follower. There are areas where I may need to change in order to improve my marriage. Help me to grow in my understanding, my perspective and my emotions so I can be a better spouse."

Actions

What specific things will you do today to work on change?

- _____
- _____
- _____

Day Seven:
Connection

Nothing is so simple that it cannot be misunderstood.
– Freeman Teague, Jr.

Two monologues don't make a dialogue.
– Jeff Daly

Before I speak, I have something important to say.
– Groucho Marx

To answer before listening is folly and shame.
– King Solomon (Proverbs 18:13)

I need to talk about kissing.

In my marriage, there are three kinds of kisses.
The "Do Not Mess Up My Lipstick" kiss.
The "Kiss Me Like You Mean It!" kiss.
The "Do You Have Another Forty Minutes?" kiss.

The "Do Not Mess Up My Lipstick" kiss is short, sweet and about ninety-six percent air. As suggested by the title, it is the preferred kiss for those times when Holly does not want me to mess up her lipstick and I do not want to wear her lipstick to work. It is casual. It is mutual. It is a polite reminder of love.

The "Kiss Me Like You Mean It!" kiss has little regard for lipstick smudging. It takes no less than ten seconds. Ten seconds may not sound like a long time, but it can seem like forever when you are in a hurry.

The "Kiss Me Like You Mean It!" kiss is all about slowing down. It is all about connection. It says, "I am never in too big of a hurry to say, I love you." This is more than ritual, and more than a casual reminder of your love. This is all about really "seeing" your spouse.

One time Holly thought we were doing the "lipstick kiss" and I said to her, "Hey, kiss me like you mean it." And so we went there. Ten seconds of being fully present for each other.

Did you see what I did there?

Holly thought, "I need to go, we are going to say good-bye, a quick kiss is perfectly appropriate in this context," but I pushed the pause button.

I called an audible.

I did it mainly because I am usually the one in a hurry. I am focused on the next moment instead of this one, but not this time.

In that "Kiss Me Like You Mean It!" request, I was telling Holly, "I just wanted to say how much I love you and how much I will be thinking about you today." It is not a "Have a Good Day" kiss, nor is it even my favorite kind (we are getting to that), but it is a kiss of true connection.

Holly loves that kiss, but I have to admit, this was not a kiss I really understood initially. For me kissing was all or nothing – the "Lipstick" kiss or the "Do You Have Another Forty Minutes?" kiss were all I really understood.

I first started to enjoy the "Kiss Me Like You Mean It!" kiss when I discovered that it often paid benefits later. (And by benefits I mean…well…you can figure that out.) However, then I realized the greatest benefit of the "Kiss Me Like You Mean It!" kiss is right there in that ten seconds – it is in the connection.

Then there is the "Do You Have Another Forty Minutes?" kiss. This is my personal favorite. This is a kiss that gets your attention. Your heart beats faster, your pheromones kick your hormones into action and your imagination awakens. There is an exchange of saliva and suddenly an unstoppable idea forms in your head:

"This could lead to something."

Yes, I am talking about sex. Or at least some serious making-out. A quick aside – this is probably the sort of kiss single people should avoid, because once you are in the middle of this kiss, you are already leaning over the edge. It is difficult to step away from the ledge when you are already falling, but for married couples? Yes! Yes! Yes! This is a very good kiss. It is more than a polite acknowledgment of love, it is more than a connection that says, "I see you" – it is a kiss that says, "I not only love you and see you...I want you." It is about desire and it is about connecting in the most intimate of ways.

Kissing is connection, but connection does not happen if we are not listening.

If I do not hear how anxious or pressed for time Holly is and try to start a "Do You Have Another Forty Minutes?" kiss, unrealistic expectations take the place of connection. If she misses my clues about wanting to enjoy a more intimate connection and throws me a "Lipstick" kiss without acknowledging my desire, I may find myself fighting disappointment or even resentment for the rest of the day.

The more we listen to one another the more we realize we need to connect more often. Connection reminds us how much we care about each other. We need to connect regularly to flourish.

Connecting is "being present" with your spouse; it is engagement of the eyes, the heart and the soul.

Let's face it, we all have busy lives. Whether it is work, family, hobbies, friends, or even the need for time alone, our days are packed from dawn till dusk. It is just not possible to find more time in the day, but it is possible to use the time we have in a way that honors our marriage.

Start by taking fifteen minutes a day to talk. I do not mean talk while the television is on or while staring at your iPads or smart phones. I mean face to face, without distraction. Or go for a walk and hold hands.

Ask questions that beg thoughtful responses. Ask questions like,

"What was the best thing about your day?"

"What frustrated you about the day?"

Or if you are talking before the day gets going: "What are you most looking forward to today?" What are you most dreading?"

Invite your spouse to talk about his or her feelings or about the challenges ahead. Then, just listen. Listening is harder than it seems. Men (in particular) are always queuing up a response when their wives are still sharing. That is not listening – that is interrupting. Yes, even if you do not say a word of what you are thinking, planning your response in the middle of a spouse's heartfelt sharing is interruption. I will say it here just for the record: you do not have to fill every second with talking in order to have a conversation with your spouse. Sometimes thoughtful silence, especially after hearing someone's heart, is more meaningful than jumping right in with analysis or answers.

To really connect you have to learn to listen. *Really listen.* It is not always easy and for many of us it is unfamiliar, but it is crucial. Really listening means resisting the temptation to prepare what you are going to say next. It means letting go of the need to correct or defend your statements. It means giving your spouse your *full* attention. When two people are talking, no one is listening.

> *Two monologues don't make a dialogue.*
> – Jeff Daly

Fifteen minutes sharing and listening. At first that might seem like a lot (I am speaking to you, husbands), but it will not be long before you are looking for more time to just connect. It is such a positive, fulfilling experience.

You may be thinking, "We have children. There is no such thing as fifteen minutes of free time."

I understand this challenge. Finding time to talk in a household with children is not easy. Do it anyway. Make it a regular part of your family routine. Call it "mommy and daddy time" and make it non-negotiable. In doing this, you model the importance of husband and wife connection. You plant a seed in your children that can grow into their own healthy "mommy and daddy time" someday. If your kids struggle with this, tie it to a promise of family time immediately following the "mommy and daddy time." Let your kids choose a whole-family activity to look forward to after you have spent your fifteen minutes alone together.

A moment ago I said, "the more we listen, the more we realize we need to connect," but there is more to connection than being a good listener. Real connection happens when we are good communicators.

This is where things get complicated.

Men communicate differently than women. I know, shocker! We men are just not that good at communication. As I have already noted, no matter how much we work at communication, we will never be as skilled at it, and as welcoming of it, as women.

Rare is the man who comes home from work and says, "If I could have a good forty-five minute conversation I would feel so much better about my day."

Understanding the differences between how men and women communicate can help us connect better. Let's look at a few examples of this.

Men Tend to Be More Literal Than Women

Okay, husbands. Let's see if this sounds familiar. You are sitting in the living room, minding your own business (aka: watching sports) when your wife speaks up out of the blue and says, "You never apologize."

At first you are a little shocked. Because of course you have apologized. You cannot recall exactly when (it is not like you write it in your calendar), but you are certain you have apologized in the past. You are absolutely convinced her statement is, in fact, inaccurate.

However, if that is how you respond when she says, "You never apologize," you are heading straight for unnecessary conflict (and maybe even a night on the couch). When she says, "You never apologize," she is not challenging you to an accounting duel – she is telling you how she feels. *In general.* (Though I would wager there is a recent event on her mind, too. Any idea what that might be?) While you are searching the database to prove her wrong, she is waiting for you to simply acknowledge her feelings. Do not turn this into an unnecessary battle. Say, "I am sorry." And mean it.

Here is another example taken from the early days of my marriage. See if you can relate.

Holly said, "Every time you touch me you just want sex."

I responded, "You cannot say 'every time'. That is simply not true. Remember that one time? Remember when I hugged you? Right after we read about your love language – physical touch. Remember that?"

Want to guess how the rest of the night went?

One more story. After we had been married a while, I finally started to understand our differences. I recognized her tendencies and my own. One day, Holly had taken a brief flight to another city. Right after she arrived at her destination, she called.

"Do you miss me?" she asked.

I looked at my watch and thought, "You only just left an hour ago. I have not had time to miss you yet." Earlier in our marriage, that is exactly what I would have said. Instead, I gave the answer she was looking for.

"Yes," I said, rather proud of myself.

She laughed. I do not think she believed me. (Women have a sixth sense about these things.) However, I do know she appreciated my efforts. That matters.

Women are Excellent Multi-taskers.

When I talk with Holly, I want her to look at me. I have a hard time believing she can be doing something else and still hear me. This leads to an inevitable exchange:

"Did you hear what I said?" I ask.

"I am listening," she says.

"Okay, what did I just say?" I protest.

And then she goes on to repeat what I said. *Verbatim.*

I have a hard time hearing what Holly is saying if I am doing something else. I give it my best shot, though. I mean, if she can do it... Right? Well, more often than not I end up looking like the distracted kid in class the teacher calls on because she suspects he is not listening.

"Did you hear what I said?" Holly asks.

"Um...was it something about dinner?" I guess.

It was not about dinner.

Women are also typically better than men at managing multiple conversations. That is the polite way of saying, "They can talk on top of each other about a dozen different things or nothing at all and be perfectly okay with that."

One day I was sitting in the kitchen with Holly, my daughter, Paris, and our friend Michelle. Notice the female to male ratio here. I started to tell one of our friends about a recent episode of The Oprah Show in which she gave each member of the audience a car. So I said to Michelle, "Did you hear what Oprah did on TV yesterday?"

"No. What happened?" she asked.

This is where I lost complete control of the conversation.

Holly said, "You didn't hear? Oh my gosh, she gave away...."

Paris joined in. Michelle started asking questions and the energy in the room shot up to one-hundred miles per hour. Words were bouncing around so fast and furious I felt like I was caught in a pinball machine. They left me in the dust.

"Oprah gave everyone a car," I finally said amidst the mayhem. I had to finish my sentence.

However, that was not the point. To many women, the interaction, the give and take and back and forth is as important as what is being said. It is where connection happens.

. . . for women.

Women Use More Words

This one does not need much explanation. It is simple math. Most men talk less than women. Therefore, husbands need to have good, patient listening skills in order to connect with their wives. Wives, on the other hand, need a different kind of patience – the kind that waits on the few words their husband will eventually offer.

In related news, I no longer say to Holly, "Guess what?" Because she always did.

"You bought a new cell phone?"

"You have a disease?"

"You just saved a lot of money on your car insurance by switching to Geico?"

I would stand in stunned silence, waiting for her to run out of words or breathe so I could get a word in. Once, when I finally had an opening to speak, I said, "In America, when a person says, 'guess what,' we respond with, 'What?' And then the person continues. You should try that sometime."

Not my best moment, but this story helps to illustrate the point. Men talk to convey information or discover facts. We do not need a lot of words for that. Women, on the other hand, have about six-million different reasons for talking and they can employ many of them at the same time.

Women Think That Hinting Is a Superior Form of Communication

Women might be right about this, but there is a small problem: Most men do not speak hint. We like things that are straightforward, clear, concise. This truth is closely related to another one: Men are not particularly good at mind-reading.

Holly used to think, "If I have to tell him I need a hug, it doesn't count." It was up to me to just know when she needed a hug.

Meanwhile, I was living according to a slightly different hug philosophy that went something like this: "Holly, I want to hug you. I want to be the man in your life who gives you all the hugs you need. Just tell me when you need one."

Obviously there was a disconnect here, and it is something we continue to work on. As it turns out, Holly wants non-sexual hugs often during the day. Non-sexual hugs? There are such things? Clearly, I still have a lot to learn. We both do.

This is probably a good time to say again, "Your mileage may vary." Much of what I am saying on these pages is based on generalizations about husbands and wives, men and women. Your situation could be the exact opposite as everyone is unique. The key is knowing how your spouse communicates and adjusting your own style of communication so it is compatible.

The Importance of Praying Together

Here are a few final thoughts for you about connection. Couples who share the same genuine faith in a personal way have stronger marriages, and couples who attend church together have stronger marriages. However, the greatest factor in the arena of faith is prayer. Research shows that couples who pray together are much stronger than couples who do not. Couples who pray together have a much better chance of working through issues and finding strength to build and maintain the great marriage they desire, rather than simply survive the difficult one they have already known.

How they pray together can be different for each couple. Some might pray daily while others might come together for prayer when they need wisdom about big decisions or help when facing one of life's many difficulties. Prayer is significant to a marriage because it is a way of bringing God into the middle of the relationship.

Prayer honors God and brings His presence into our homes.

If you really want to turn your relationship around, take a few minutes to pray today. Pray for God's guidance in work or your marriage, pray for peace in your home, healing in your marriage, protection from spiritual attacks in your relationship and forgiveness for mistakes you have made in relating to each other.

However, keep in mind that everyone prays differently. Knowing this and adapting your shared prayer time accordingly, can help you avoid the panic of an awkward time together.

Some people pray together daily – they sit across from each other and hold hands and bow their heads. If you do that, great! Holly and I do not. The "together" aspect of our prayer times is mostly in the content of our prayers. We talk about the things to pray for and then individually pray for those people and situations sometime during the day.

Gary Chapman, author of *The Five Love Languages,* has found that many men do not pray with their wives because they are uncomfortable in those moments. His solution is simple (and effective): Take five minutes for a time of shared silent prayer. Sit together, hold hands, and pray in silence.

Since you are married, you will never be short of topics for those prayer times. Why not start by praying for your marriage, for your spouse, yourself and the other members of your family. Whether in silence or aloud, these prayers not only invite God's presence into your marriage, they unite husband and wife. They build connection.

And that is a very good thing.

> *Good communication is as stimulating as black coffee, and just as hard to sleep after.*
> – Anne Morrow Lindbergh

Takeaways

List three things that stood out to you in this chapter:

1.
2.
3.

Prayer

Pray this prayer before taking the next step:
"God, help us both to communicate with more compassion and honor. Forgive me for not listening

well and help me to listen better. Help me to communicate in a way that brings unity, clarity and trust. We
need you to help us to connect in a genuine way."

Actions

*What specific things will you do today to work on
connection in your marriage?*

- _____
- _____
- _____

Day Eight:
Play

We don't stop playing because we grow old; we grow old because we stop playing.
– George Bernard Shaw

A cheerful heart is good medicine, but a crushed spirit dries up the bones.
(Proverbs 17:22)

Laugh. Laugh as much as you can. Laugh until you cry. Cry until you laugh. Keep doing it even if people are passing you on the street saying, "I can't tell if that person is laughing or crying, but either way they seem crazy, let's walk faster." Emote. It's okay. It shows you are thinking and feeling.
– Ellen DeGeneres

A ll work and no play, makes Jack a dull boy. Jack's marriage is in trouble.

Marriage takes work. A great marriage takes a lot of work. I think by Day Eight, that is becoming rather obvious. I hope it is equally obvious that the work is worth the effort, but if you are not yet convinced, this chapter should do the trick.

When I say, "marriage takes work," I do not want you to picture hard labor. Yes, there are seasons when it feels like all you do is move big rocks from one place to another, but mostly the work I am talking about serves a greater purpose. Have you discovered that purpose yet? It is to enjoy your spouse; to enjoy your shared lives together.

However, it happens to all of us – the slow decay of play. Life gets busy and hard and well, we forget to have fun. Or perhaps it is more accurate to say we forget to *make time* for fun. It feels weird (and a little sad) to have to write these words, but I am going to do it anyway. This sticky note is for you: "Remember to have fun." Attach it to your bathroom mirror, the refrigerator, the TV, the kitchen table, the dog, your wallet. Virtually, if not literally.

In our first years of marriage, Holly and I were struggling a bit so we went to a marriage retreat. At one point the speaker asked the women to stand and "say one thing that you really love about your husband." The first few women stood up and said things like:

> *My husband is really handsome.*
> *He has a great body.*
> *My husband is really intelligent – I love that about him."*

Then Holly stood up. I was on the edge of my seat, wondering if she would choose my good looks or my intelligence, or break the rules and mention both. She said:

> *He makes me laugh.*

My ego deflated for a moment, but then the speaker said, "What a great quality! That is so important to a strong marriage."

He was right. Now that we have been married nearly thirty years, I have noticed how important that quality is in our relationship. My body may not be what it once was, but my sense of humor is in great shape.

Couples with a sense of humor have a lot going for them. The ability to laugh at yourself, to not take yourself so seriously, is a sign of emotional health. A good sense of humor is also an invaluable tool in disarming tense moments. So it has many benefits.

But let's get back to the point. Holly and I went to that marriage retreat because we were struggling. One thing we learned there was the value of a sense of humor and having fun.

We now recognize the moments that open the door to laughter. We set aside time to just "play" and we value that time. We have date nights. We have learned not to hurry on to the "important" things, and that laughter might actually be one of the most important ingredients of a healthy marriage.

Jay Leno was offering some solid marriage advice when he said, "You can't stay mad at someone who makes you laugh."

After we had children, we made sure we planned two vacations whenever possible: one with the family and one just for the two of us. Some years it was just a few days away, but those few days?

Totally worth it.

We like to have fun. We work hard, so why not play hard. We found, though, that the key was to be intentional. If you just go about your day with only a vague idea of making time for play, you will probably come to the end of your day, your week or your life and wonder where that time went. So schedule time for nonsense. Go to the beach. Go out for ice cream. Play tennis. Play Angry Birds. Play table games – we like to play backgammon together. Relax a little. Relax a lot. Find something to laugh about.

Here is one important tip: Be open to the things your spouse enjoys. It may stretch you a bit to visit a museum if that is not your thing, but your spouse, who loves museums, will love you more for going along. (It goes without saying, but please do not use your dislike of museums as an opportunity to complain. You are spending time together, and whatever you do together can be fun if you allow it to be.)

I happen to love major league baseball! Watching the Yankees, Dodgers, summer nights at the ballpark, now that is my idea of fun.

My wife has discovered that she likes it too. She cheers with me. She cheers louder than me. She asks intelligent questions about the players and what is going on. I love it that she did not metaphorically pat me on the head and say, "you go ahead and enjoy your little sports thing." Instead, she took a risk and dove right in because it was something I loved.

In the first year of our marriage, I took Holly to her first game at Dodger Stadium. We were having a great time. In the third inning, I got up to get hotdogs (do not judge until you have tried one at the ballpark – there is nothing like 'em) and drinks and other snacks. When I returned with the food, she was standing there with a big grin on her face – and holding a baseball.

She told me what happened.

While I was waiting in line for our food, she had been talking to the people around her and enjoying the camaraderie that is the lifeblood of the ballpark. All of a sudden everyone stood and reached up in the air yelling, "Look out, here it comes!"

She covered her head with both arms for protection. In all the excitement and chaos, the foul ball bounced around and rolled right up to her feet. She reached down and picked it up.

I have been going to baseball games since I was twelve years old. I wore a glove to the games back then, in hopes that I might snag a foul ball. Okay, I still bring a glove with me to this day. But even when

I did not wear a glove, catching a foul was my greatest baseball-related dream.

Holly got one at her very first game. Because of this, I know for a fact God has a sense of humor. He is a God of good moments. He knows the importance of play.

Playfulness is contagious. Holly has a black belt in playfulness! She teases. She starts play fights. She jokes with total strangers. I am a little more reserved – I prefer my wit dry – but I do like to have fun, too.

One area in a marriage that requires hard work is finances. The way we manage money and the way we think about it is often the source of disagreements and arguments. Financial problems – and the way we try to solve them – steals joy out of relationships and life out of marriage. Financial problems are among the top reasons couples divorce.

So keep your finances in mind when trying to play harder or play more. Remember your budget limitations, or your laughter could turn to tears in no time. Find ways to laugh together even when things are tight financially.

Learning to communicate about money, hopes, desires and expectations honestly and without blame is so important to a good marriage. I highly recommend Dave Ramsey's *Total Money Make Over* for all couples. Following Dave's sage advice can help assure that finances will be a means of bringing joy into your relationship and not pain.

One night we joined a bunch of other couples for dinner at a friend's house. There were about eight couples in all. After dinner, I offered to help put whipped cream on the pies we were about to serve. We were just talking and enjoying preparing the dessert when one of Holly's good friends accidentally sprayed some whipping cream on me.

Without hesitation, I turned and sprayed right back. She was stunned for a second but retaliated a moment later. Then it happened. The room erupted into a whipped cream fight. This was totally out of character for me but so much fun. People were running from the kitchen and laughing. The fight probably only lasted about two minutes, but it gave us a whole evening of entertainment. We still enjoy memories of the delectable chaos. That is the thing about playfulness and fun; it is great in the moment and almost as fun in the memory.

Playfulness can be both intoxicating and exciting. It nurtures the part of us that still feels like a kid.

You cannot fake playfulness, however. Unless it comes from within, it does not really count. I have already mentioned how important it is to be intentional about making time for play. Here is the best thing about that – the more you do this, the better you will become at spontaneous playfulness; and some of the best playful moments happen spontaneously.

Laughter has a powerful effect on your health and well-being. A good laugh relieves tension and stress, elevates mood, enhances creativity and problem-solving ability, and provides a quick energy boost. Even more importantly, laughter brings people together. Mutual laughter and play are essential ingredients of strong, healthy relationships. By making a conscious effort to incorporate more humor and play into your daily interactions, you can improve the quality of your love relationships, as well as your connections with co-workers, family members, and friends.

I have already mentioned that the couple who prays together, stays together. So, too, the couple that *plays* together.

Learn to play.

Takeaways

List three things that stood out to you in this chapter:

1.
2.
3.

Prayer

Pray this prayer before taking the next step:

"Marriage is hard work. We need your help as we work on our relationship. Help us to find the joy in it, too. Lord we need your joy in our hearts and in our marriage. Help us to laugh again. Help us to play more.

Where there is sorrow or sadness in my soul, I ask you to replace it with real joy."

Actions

What specific things will you do today to work on play?

- _____
- _____
- _____

Day Nine:
Needs

Every one of us needs to show how much we care for each other and, in the process, care for ourselves.
– Princess Diana

Do nothing out of selfish ambition or vain conceit. Rather, in humility value others above yourselves, not looking to your own interests but each of you to the interests of the others.
– Apostle Paul

I married him for a green card. We had a really great, caring relationship; it just obviously wasn't right for me.
– Portia de Rossi

If your marriage is all about meeting your needs, you have got it backwards. Like so many other couples, your marriage will be lacking. You will become frustrated. The better you become at meeting your spouse's needs, the better your marriage will be.

"But what about my needs?" you ask. That is a great question! Jesus gave some clues about the secret to great relationships: *Do for other people whatever you would like to have them do for you. Give and it will be given to you.*

Then how do you turn it all around? How do you put your spouse first? You begin by embracing this truth: Behind every complaint or frustration is an unmet need.

I discovered this when I was doing marriage counseling many years ago. On one particular day, I met with a couple who was going through a ton of challenges. They were so far apart in their relationship I had to look at my appointment book to make sure I had not somehow scheduled the wife with somebody else's husband by mistake.

Counseling these two was testing my abilities, pushing me beyond what I had been trained for. I was trying to sound intelligent and be discerning, but inside I was thinking, "I don't know what to tell you. You are a mess! That is probably not helpful, is it? God, help me out here. What do I say? How can I help? Is there any hope?"

God must have been listening, because I came up with an idea…and it worked.

I said, "Mrs. Wife, I want you to tell me five things that you need in this relationship. Don't tell me things you need your husband to do. This is not time to complain about all the ways your husband is failing. This is a list of your needs, things that are important to you, feelings you want to feel in your marriage." I called this list the "High Five."

I wrote down her list.

"Mr. Husband, tell me five things *you* need in this marriage."

I wrote those down, too. The lists included things like, "…to feel valued, to feel loved, to feel respected, to feel admired, to feel important."

I started with the first item on Mrs. Wife's list. I said to Mr. Husband, "Your wife says she needs to feel valued. Do you think that is a legitimate need?"

"Yes," he replied.

"If you knew how to help her to feel that deep inside, would you be willing to try?"

"Yes," he said again.

I asked Mrs. Wife, "What are some things he could do that would help you feel that sense of value?"

"Well maybe if we could have a conversation where he really listens to me, just listens. He doesn't need to have all the answers when we talk. I don't always need answers. And it doesn't have to be a long conversation – just fifteen or twenty minutes. That would tell me he cares about how I'm feeling. That would be so huge for me," she said.

"Mr. Husband, are you willing to try that?" He said yes. "Then make a commitment to have two or three of these conversations during the week. You agreed that her need to feel valued is legitimate. This is your opportunity to show her you mean it."

Then we looked at Mr. Husband's list and did the same thing for the first item. We did not try to tackle all five in one day. We just started with one or two for each of them in order to build positive momentum in the healing of their relationship.

You are a step ahead of me again, aren't you? Yes, it is homework time for you. I want you to write down your own "High Five" lists. This is not an exercise only for couples who are in crisis – it is a great way to make a good marriage even better.

What are five things you need from your marriage? Remember, your values are your fingerprint. Consider connecting your needs, desires and decisions to your values. Here is a sample list to get you thinking:

> *I need to feel...*
> *Like I am the most important person in your world.*
> *That you care about what I am saying.*
> *That you would change your plans if I needed you.*
> *That you care about what is important to me.*
> *That you would protect me.*

Then ask yourself, "What practical things can my spouse do to help me feel this way?" Be specific whenever possible and try to focus on the positive

– do not let this conversation turn into a gripe session. Listen to what your spouse is saying. Then make plans to take action wherever you can to help your spouse experience his or her "High Five."

> *Each of you should look not only to your own interests, but also to the interests of others.*
> (Philippians 2:4)

Holly and I tried the "High Five" experiment. Holly's list included, "I need to feel that you care about what I am saying."

"Ok, I want to do that." I said with enthusiasm. "Um…how do I do that?"

"I want you to look at me and listen when I am talking to you," She said. "No cell phone, no remote control – just look at me."

I said, "This is great because that is what I want from you too. I need to know you are listening. I mean *really* listening to me. So I want you to stop what you are doing and look at me when I talk."

"I don't need to, I'm a woman," she said. "I can do more than one thing at a time. I can do like three things at a time and I know exactly what you're saying."

I know this is true. I mentioned it in an earlier chapter as evidence of our differences. Nevertheless, the more I thought about it the more I realized it irritated me.

"I know Holly, but I can't do that so it's hard for me to believe that you can. I just want you to look at me," I said, sticking to my needs.

She smiled that knowing sweet smile, then agreed to do this because she loves me and wants me to feel valued, too.

Then she said, "So what did I ask you to do?"

Awkward but familiar silence.

"What did you ask me to do? You mean before we started talking about this? I was listening. I really was. And I was looking right at you, and...um...can you give me a clue?"

We have been working on this for about eighteen years. I think we are getting better at it. It is only a matter of time before we get to the third item on our "High Five" lists.

I shared this personal story for a reason, though. The "High Five" exercise is a great way to learn more about your spouse, and it is a great step toward a better, more fulfilling marriage. But even if you do everything your spouse and you agree on, things will not suddenly be perfect. We do not always get everything right. Yet the more we discover about what our spouse needs to feel loved, the better we will be able to love our spouse.

Isn't that what is most important?

There is one more important thing to explore, and it is a biggie. **Day Ten** is coming, and it is time for you and your spouse to dream again.

Takeaways

List three things that stood out to you in this chapter:

1.
2.
3.

Prayer

Pray this prayer before taking the next step:

"God, show me how to understand my spouse's needs. Help me see how I can contribute toward meeting those needs. Forgive me for the times I have only thought about my needs instead of giving my whole heart to care about my spouse's needs."

Actions

What specific things will you do today to work on meeting your spouse's needs?

- _____
- _____
- _____

Day Ten:
Dreams

Dream no small dreams for they have no power to move the hearts of men.
– Johann Wolfgang von Goethe

All our dreams can come true, if we have the courage to pursue them.
- Walt Disney

Hope deferred makes the heart sick, but a dream fulfilled is a tree of life.
– King Solomon (Proverbs 13:12 NLT)

Sitting in Starbucks one day I was talking with some friends, a husband and wife who were struggling in their relationship. They thought it might be over for them. Let's just call them Jenny and Daniel.

Jenny said, "We used to talk about what we were going to do with our life. We walked on the beach, held hands and imagined possibilities for our future. It was so exciting. Maybe we were immature or naïve then, but now we're just struggling to keep up with life's demands. Those days seem like a distant memory."

"I love her. I really do." Daniel assured us. "But our lives have gotten so complicated and overwhelming. I feel like we've lost something. I don't know where we went wrong."

Kristen and Justin struggled with this, too. After being married seven years, they moved to Los Angeles. The move gave each of them unique opportunities to pursue their individual interests. Justin was pursuing a music career, collaborating with other artists, song writing and doing studio work. Kristen was actively researching and becoming more aware of social injustice. Over a span of a few months they shared fewer common interests and found it more difficult to spend quality time together.

In the middle of a big fight, Kristen said, "You are not the man I married," to which Justin, replied,

"You are not the same person either." It was during this disagreement that they both became aware of the significant changes that were occurring within each other – new dreams, desires and wants that they had failed to communicate or understand.

This is not a new story. Holly and I had our own dreams. You had yours, but life happens, and life has a way of hijacking our dreams.

Problems arise. We run into roadblocks. We take detours. We head in different directions. We have children, buy a home, and change jobs. For many couples, these things conspire to steal the color from their shared dreams. Those dreams – once the life-blood of the relationship – fade to black and white.

Remember when you used to talk about those dreams? Your face would light up, your excitement level would rise. "Someday, we'll..." you would begin, fully believing that together you would accomplish so many things.

Proverbs 29:18 says, "Where there is no vision, the people perish." (KJV). King Solomon was on to something there.

Coaches know about this principle. Leaders realize that if the vision is not clear the followers lose focus. But many couples do not understand just how crucial vision is to their relationship. Without vision, the marriage can perish.

As we go through life, our focus shifts from dreaming to surviving. This is not a big surprise. When life demands we put all of our mental energies into sorting through the challenges and frustrations in our relationships, work and living conditions, shared dreams start to look like luxuries we cannot afford. We stop dreaming of what we will do someday and try to convince ourselves that what we are doing today is good enough. Then, in those rare moments when we *do* dream, we do so separately. This can be as devastating to a relationship as not dreaming at all.

Kristen and Justin finally understood more about their own challenges when two friends offered this explanation for their impending divorce: "We just grew apart." That sounded just a little too close to home. Kristen and Justin realized they had been pursuing dreams as individuals instead of as a married couple.

"This was a defining moment for our marriage," says Kristen. "We had to find a way to grow together as we pursued the dreams God placed in our hearts, and take the time to pursue one another like we did when we were dating. We weren't the same people that we were when we were married – and that was a good thing! We just had to get to know each other once again – we had to learn to ask the right questions.

"Instead of only asking 'how was your day?' we started asking 'what is God showing you' or 'what is the dream that God is putting on your heart?' We started looking for ways we could support each other, and define what was meaningful to us as a couple. Weekly date nights became a high priority again, and we began to ask the question, 'how can we accomplish this together?'"

For Kristen and Justin, asking these questions led them to many new shared dreams: going to Africa, becoming foster parents, building God's House, ministering to young people and pursuing adoption.

Remember when you used to dream together? Go back to that place for a moment. Embrace possibilities together. Think about what you could accomplish. If there were no limits, what would you do? Where would you go? How would you make a difference?

I recently talked this through with Holly. I said, "Holly, when we got married, what were we talking about and imagining for our life? What were we thinking?"

She smiled and rolled her eyes, "I have asked myself that question many times. What were we thinking?"

"Ok, let me re-phrase the question. What did we dream about? What were our goals?"

Silence.

A long silence.

Too long of a silence.

I tried to move the conversation forward. "I wanted to grow a big church in LA and for you to get a role in a TV series...so we could pay for this big church idea. Okay, that's just a guess. Maybe we didn't have dreams back then. To be honest, I can't remember what we were dreaming. We just were in love and just wanted to make passionate love to each other and have fun. "

This may or may not been our entire plan.

"Our dreams have evolved," she finally said. "What's important is that we've grown up, we've gotten wiser and we're more aware of the importance of the dreams we now have."

"Oh, that's good." I interjected. "I'm going to put that in the book as if I said it."

She ignored me, then continued.

"Our dreams are to be together for the rest of our lives and be in love with each other. They are to be around long enough to be involved in our grandchildren's lives. We are living our lives to honor God. We are dedicated to building the local church. I believe God has given me a mission to bring value to women, that you have a passion to help widows and orphans and that we are to support each other in doing it. . . ."

"This is great," I said. "I'm writing it down. I mean, I know it in here [I pointed to my heart] but I like the way you said it. Is it wrong for us to put something in here about baseball?"

"...And to help as many people as we can to reach their God-given dreams." She concluded.

"Have I told you lately how amazing you are? You are awesome." I said. "Do you have another forty minutes?"

She just shook her head and walked away.

Antoine de Saint-Exupery wrote, "The secret to lasting love isn't gazing at each other but focusing together in the same direction." This is the reason dreaming is critical to marital success and fulfillment.

This leads to one final thought. In a way, we have come full circle. Remember what I said in the introduction? True love is all about sacrifice.

My job, as a husband, is to help my wife reach *her* goals and dreams. When I read the scriptures that tell me I am the "head" of the relationship, that does not mean everything is supposed to go my way. My job as the head is to ensure that my wife accomplishes what God has designed her to do.

I do not want to stand before God on that very important day when we all stand before Him at the end of our life and hear Him say, "Philip, what were you doing? I brought this amazing woman into your life but she could not do what I prepared for her because you were too selfish and insecure. You treated her like it was all about you."

So I asked Holly, "What do you believe God wants you to do? I want to help you do it. What are your dreams? What are your goals? How can I help you?"

Husbands, ask your wives how you can help them reach for their God-given dreams.

Wives, ask your husbands the same question.

Both of you watch out for the dream stealers. You know these well – weariness, financial problems, health issues, bitterness, loss of hope, spiritual stagnation, unbelief, fear.

Avoid Comparison

One more Dream Stealer: comparison (or jealousy).

Do not let comparison steal your dreams. I have already shared how Holly's background was much different than mine. At times, I have struggled with that. I have even felt a little bitter, perhaps that is aimed at God rather than Holly, but it is an unhealthy thing wherever I am pointing.

Holly has had so many great opportunities given to her. Sometimes it seems like every door opens automatically for her – like the ones at the grocery store. (Do I need to remind you that she got a foul ball at her first baseball game?) Meanwhile, I struggle for every little breakthrough.

This makes me think that if we approached our life together as a competition, I would lose. If I compared my circumstances to hers, I would come up short. That is only half of the truth; if we approached our life together as a competition, we *both* would lose.

When we were first married we struggled like most couples to make money. I was working two jobs and neither was bringing in much. She had been acting and was making some money here and there, but the residuals were getting smaller. I told her, "Holly you're going to have to get a job."

She said, "Okay, but first, I want to go on a game show."

"What? That is nothing like a job. What I'm talking about is going to work and getting a paycheck that you have agreed on."

However, it was one of her dreams. We talked about it for a while, and eventually agreed she should do it. I figured that once it was out of her system, she would be happy to get a "real" job.

She went on the show called Password.

And won $23,000!

In one day.

This was the 1980s, way back when gas was just a dollar and a quarter a gallon, so that was a lot of money. More than I had made in my job so far that year.

Holly not only got to enjoy one of her dreams, we both got to enjoy the fact that she was really good at Password.

When you get back to dreaming together and celebrating each other's visions for the future, all kinds of crazy, good things can happen. Your spouse might even win a bunch of cash on a game show.

You will also be winning something far more valuable – you will be winning a better marriage. You just cannot put a price on that.

Pray. Ask God to guide you. Ask God to give you a dream for your marriage and for your life that will honor Him.

> *Now to Him who is able to do immeasurably more than all we ask or imagine, according to his power that is at work within us...* (Ephesians 3:20)

Let your imagination go.

God is the Dream Maker. He makes Heaven's dreams for our life a reality.

A few thoughts from fellow dreamers:

> *There are only two ways to live your life. One is as though nothing is a miracle. The other is as though everything is a miracle.*
> – Albert Einstein

It is never too late to be what you might have been.
– George Eliot

And in the end, it's not the years in your life that count. It's the life in your years.
– Abraham Lincoln

Logic will get you from A to B. Imagination will take you everywhere.
– Albert Einstein

Look up!
And look ahead.

May your fountain be blessed. . .
(Proverbs 5:18-19)

Takeaways

List three things that stood out to you in this chapter:
   1.
   2.
   3.

Prayer

Pray this prayer before taking the next step:
"God, we want our lives and our marriage to honor you. Help us to dream the dreams you have for us. Breathe life into our hearts and our imagination.

Bring your blessing into our home – on earth as it is in Heaven."

Actions

What specific things will you do today to work toward fulfilling your dreams?

- _____
- _____
- _____

Day Eleven
Repeat

Patient endurance is what you need now, so that you will continue to do God's will. Then you will receive all that he has promised.
(Hebrews 10:36)

When you realize you want to spend the rest of your life with somebody, you want the rest of your life to start as soon as possible.
– Billy Crystal

It ain't over till it's over.
– Yogi Berra

Day Eleven. I know, the title of this book is "How to Turn Your Marriage Around in 10 Days." So why is there a Day Eleven?

Because in marriage, there is a Day Twelve, and a Day Thirteen, and a Day Fourteen, and, and, and...

The subtitle of this chapter says it all: *Repeat.*

Keep doing all the good things you are learning. Listen well. Forgive generously. Dream loud and often. Persist. Grow. Learn.

You might be tempted to think of the last ten days as an experiment. Something you are trying out to see if it works for your marriage.

I am going to challenge you to think differently. Experiments are momentary, temporary. Instead of an experiment, consider the past ten days a re-framing of how you do marriage. It is not just a new way of thinking – it is a new way of living.

Leadership guru, John Maxwell, says, "Momentum solves 80% of your problems." I believe it. When you begin to turn things around, keep it going. When the environment of your marriage begins to shift, you are going in the right direction. Fan the flames.

Nevertheless, here is an important warning: *be careful not to use this book as a wedge in your relationship or to pressure your spouse to change his or her ways.* The book is meant to help both husband and wife work on their marriage. I hope you and your spouse are on the same page here – that you both want to turn your marriage around. Your job is to work on all these things in *you*, not to guilt your spouse into doing them.

Here is something you *can* do for your spouse – you can offer encouragement. Specific and genuine encouragement is one of the most powerful dynamics in any relationship. We are all hungry for encouragement. We gravitate toward it.

Encouragement is like a magnet. In Proverbs, King Solomon shares an allegory that tells of a man who falls victim to an affair. He writes, "So she seduced him with her pretty speech and enticed him with her flattery." (Proverbs 7:21 NLT) It was not her beauty that tempted him, it was her words. Of course, I am not about to condone her action here, but the message is clear: *Words have power.*

Encouragement may be one of the greatest things we can give our spouse. It is also a great way to shore up a marriage. I am convinced that affairs often begin because of a lack of personal encouragement from our spouse. Solomon's words serve as fair warning about this, don't you think?

Hebrews 3:13 challenges us to "…encourage one another daily." The key here is "daily." Words of encouragement and "I love you" have the same shelf life – about twenty-four hours. Our souls crave constant encouragement – and in a marriage, the primary source for meeting that need should be our spouse.

Encourage your spouse's strengths and attempts at improvement. Be careful not to offer backhanded compliments in lieu of sincere encouragement.

Saying, "You don't look as chubby in that dress as you used to" is not the same as, "I love that you're so committed to exercise – I could learn a thing or two from you."

Remember to offer encouragement for past accomplishments, too.

Holly encourages me like no one else. She sees things in me that even I cannot see. When she compliments me it weighs ten times more than the average compliment from a friend or stranger. The difference? She knows me – and because she knows me, every sincere word matters more. A stranger can tell me, "I loved what you said in your sermon" and that will make me feel good, but if Holly says the same thing, it makes me feel rare, loved, and seen. That is one of the greatest opportunities spouses have – *to make each other feel rare, precious and special.*

In addition to coming from a place of sincerity, encouragement needs to be positive, uplifting.

When our children were learning to walk we would stand them up against the wall and say, "Come to Daddy," and they would take a wobbly step or two. Holly and I would cheer, clap, and say "Good boy" or "What a big girl." We encouraged each and every step. "Wow, look at all the steps you took! What a great job!"

This works! It is a tried and true method of encouragement, passed down from generation to generation. But what if we used a different method – one of criticizing and critiquing every little thing.

"You call that walking? You're doing it wrong. You'll never get anywhere in life walking like that!"

I think you would agree that method probably would not be as successful. Even if it did work, the child would forever associate walking with criticism and "not living up to expectations."

Hmm...I wonder how many times we have fallen prey to this kind of "encouragement" in our marriages?

Jim was not spending much time with his young son, Taylor. Michelle, his wife of six years, asked him to spend more time with Taylor. Jim gave this the ol' college try, but his results did not live up to his effort. After returning from a friend's house one day, his wife confronted him. "That's all you could come up with, to take him to your friend's house? I wanted you to spend some *quality* father-son time."

Jim might not have made the best decision there, but he was trying. In his mind, he was doing exactly what his wife wanted. However, when she criticized him instead of acknowledging his attempt, he walked away defeated. I wonder if he ever tried again. I am certain he was afraid to, because criticism shuts us down.

Remember this: You are not your spouse's gymnastics coach. You are not training for the Olympics. You are your spouse's support system – the best possible source of confidence your spouse will ever know.

Genuine encouragement has power.

Do not let any unwholesome talk come out of your mouths, but only what is helpful for building others up according to their needs, that it may benefit those who listen. (Ephesians 4:29)

Do not withhold good from those who deserve it when it's in your power to help them. (Proverbs 3:27)

This takes us to the end of Day Eleven. Are you ready for Days Twelve through Twelve-Thousand?

If you do what others will not do, you can have what others will not; a lasting, satisfying, and beautiful marriage.

We live in a society full of hares. Does anyone remember that the tortoise won the race?

Thanks for committing to turning your marriage around. Thanks for doing all this hard work. It is worth it.

Look at all the steps you took! What a great job!

Now keep walking.

———⁓⁓⁓———

For more information about Philip Wagner and
other resources
www.PhilipWagner.com
www.facebook.com/OfficialPhilipWagner
Twitter @PhilipWagnerLA
www.OasisLA.org

CPSIA information can be obtained at www.ICGtesting.com
Printed in the USA
BVOW081608091012

302554BV00001B/1/P